INTRODUCTION

❧

I first became aware of the First World War when I was taken as a child to the Imperial War Museum. I don't know how old I was, but I remember being powerfully moved by a photograph of blinded and gassed British soldiers stumbling in single file through the battlefields. The image lingers today. Why and how had this happened? – these are questions to which I'm still seeking the answers.

In this I'm not alone – the reading rooms at the National Archives at Kew are full of people tracing their fathers and grandfathers who served during the First World War, and who are often profoundly moved by what they find. According to the Belgian historian Guy Gruwez, writing in *At the Going Down of the Sun*:

Interest in the Great War was not rekindled by great national ceremonies of remembrance, nor by learned academic works detailing the military and political developments of the war years. The gradual reawakening of interest in the Great War – which began in the 1970s and has grown dramatically during the past 10 years – owes almost everything to the desire of ordinary men and women to understand what happened to their own relatives and their own region. Perhaps they stumbled across some old documents or the diary of their grandfather. Perhaps they became curious – and later fascinated – by the names and nationalities on the headstones in the cemeteries that litter the countryside around Ypres. In this manner the history of a long, half-forgotten war became entwined with their own personal history; it was here that men fought and died; it was my grandfather who stood on this spot; the men and the women caught up in the war were just like me, with the same hopes and fears, the same passions and desires.

Popular interest in the war has been spurred by the intense media interest in the few surviving veterans (who must have seemed to many viewers to have been time travellers from another age) and with the release of service records by the Public Record Office which allowed family and military historians to discover for the first time what their fathers and grandfathers really did in France and Flanders.

This book is intended as a guide for people who want to know more about an ancestor's wartime service, or the local men who marched away never to return, or how the war affected the local village. It assumes no prior knowledge of military history or of the archives themselves, but I hope that more experienced researchers will also find it of use. The whole point is to encourage you, the reader, to get out of your armchair to find out for yourself.

However, it does not pretend to be a history of the war itself. There are a large number of excellent general histories (see the bibliography for a number of suggestions). Nor indeed can the book claim to be comprehensive, but I hope that a recommended book or archival source might provide a lead to be followed up.

Unfortunately, the war has been the subject of much ignorant myth-making. The most pernicious are the old accusation of 'Lions led by Donkeys' and that the whole war was a ghastly mistake that saw the senseless slaughter of millions of young lives. These are trotted out each Armistice Day by the media, yet TV producers and their researchers forget that the British and their allies actually won the war. Indeed, the so-called 'hundred days' from mid-August 1918 to the armistice in November was almost certainly the greatest British military victory ever. As I hope you will discover, the truth is a lot more complicated than is usually presented on television. Military historians still argue bitterly about the effectiveness of Sir Douglas Haig and the British High Command. Meanwhile, family and local historians are amazed that individual soldiers might actually have enjoyed their time in the services. While the conditions in the front line were undoubtedly hellish, not every day was like the Battle of Passchendaele. In many parts of the line an informal policy of 'live and let live' ensured relative comfort for men on both sides. If nothing else, I hope this book will encourage you to discover what went on for yourself.

There are introductory chapters about where to get started and the armed services during the war and how to conduct various kinds of research. Although it is often forgotten, the First World War was fought not entirely by the British (helped by the gallant ANZACs at Gallipoli),

TRACING
YOUR
FIRST WORLD WAR
ANCESTORS

TRACING
YOUR
FIRST WORLD WAR
ANCESTORS

— SIMON FOWLER —

COUNTRYSIDE BOOKS
NEWBURY BERKSHIRE

First published 2003
© Simon Fowler 2003

COUNTRYSIDE BOOKS
3 Catherine Road
Newbury, Berkshire

To view our complete range of books,
please visit us at
www.countrysidebooks.co.uk

ISBN 1 85306 791 1

Typeset by Textype, Cambridge
Produced through MRM Associates Ltd., Reading
Printed by Woolnough Bookbinding Ltd., Irthlingborough

CONTENTS

❦

The statue of Earl Haig at Edinburgh Castle. Sir Douglas Haig, became Commander in Chief of the British Expeditionary Force in December 1915. His generalship still excites controversy today.

but also by troops from across the Empire as well as American, Belgian, Italian, Portuguese, Russian and above all French soldiers. There were also, of course, millions of brave Germans (including my own maternal grandfather), Austrian and Turkish troops. So there is a chapter about how to find out more about some of these men. Lastly, there are the appendices, including addresses of archives and museums, suggestions for further reading and a guide to visiting the battlefields for yourself.

At the risk of annoying Flemish nationalists, place-names here use the form (normally French) in which they have long been familiar, first to the Tommies themselves and later to visitors to the Western Front (most notably Ypres, for example, instead of Ieper). As the book was being prepared, the Public Record Office (PRO) became the National Archives (NA), rather a shock for those of us long used to the old name. Where possible the new title has been used throughout, although the old usage may occasionally have slipped through.

As always I am grateful for the encouragement of Nicholas Battle and his team at Countryside Books in writing this book. Over the years students at my family history classes and lectures, together with letters from readers of *Family History Monthly*, have raised questions, some of which are answered here. Errors and omissions are, of course, my own.

Simon Fowler

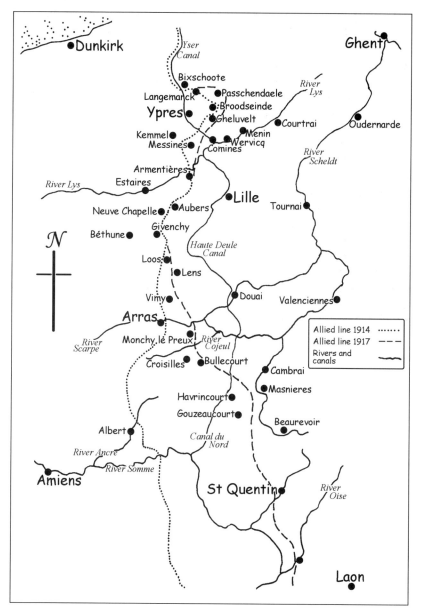

The Western Front, 1914–1918.

In Flanders Fields

In Flanders fields the poppies blow
Between the crosses, row on row,
That mark our place; and in the sky
The larks, still bravely singing, fly
Scarce heard amid the guns below.
We are the Dead. Short days ago
We lived, felt dawn, saw sunset glow,
Loved, and were loved, and now we lie
In Flanders fields.
Take up our quarrel with the foe:
To you from failing hands we throw
The torch, be yours to hold it high.
If ye break faith with us who die
We shall not sleep, though poppies grow
In Flanders fields.

John McCrae (1872–1918)

1

GETTING STARTED

Even though the First World War lasted only a little over four years and there is almost nobody now alive who can remember it, it continues to fascinate historians – professional and amateur alike. Most people are drawn to the subject by a desire to find out what happened to an individual, often a father or grandfather, during their military service, or are moved by the names on a local war memorial and want to know more about these men. It is on these personal histories that this book largely concentrates, rather than the great policy issues of the day.

WHERE TO START

The best place to begin your research is to work out what you know already. Write down definite facts as well as anything that you are not absolutely sure of. Of course it is pretty important to know which service (Army, Royal Navy, Royal Air Force) he was with. It is very useful to have to hand:

- which unit he served with: that is, regiment or corps for the Army, ship(s) in the Navy, and squadron in the Air Force
- when he served and when he was discharged
- date of death if killed in action or died of wounds
- where he served – usually, but certainly not always, the Western Front (usually referred to as France and Flanders in the records).

In an ideal world you would also know:

- his regimental number (there may have been several)
- what injuries or disabilities resulted from his war service. They may

A group of soldiers at a training camp. It should be possible to identify their regiment from the distinctive cap badges.

have been physical such as an artificial leg or shrapnel in the body, or psychological – perhaps he was plagued by recurring nightmares?
- the medals he was awarded.

When I researched the war service of my great-uncle Stanley, all I knew was that he had served in the Army (in, possibly, the Royal Fusiliers) and died shortly before the armistice was signed in 1918. I later found that he was actually Henry Philip Stanley Crozier, 18th Battalion, King's Royal Rifle Corps, who died on 26th October 1918 and is buried near Courtrai in Belgium.

This book should help you follow up these leads and give you ideas about where else you could look for information. Once you start, you might be pleasantly surprised about what you can find out.

IDENTIFYING OLD PHOTOGRAPHS

Many families have photographs of men in uniform. With some effort and a bit of luck you should be able to find more about the man and his service from looking carefully at the picture. The first thing to do is to try to identify his regiment from a cap badge or belt buckle. Chevrons on the sleeves of his uniform would indicate that he was a non-commissioned officer, while other patches might denote the number of times he was wounded and the division to which his unit belonged. Over his heart should be the medal ribbons, or possibly the medals themselves. Pips on his shoulder and a smarter cut of uniform would suggest that the sitter is an officer.

However, with the bewildering number of badges, stripes and other insignia it is easy to get confused. Fortunately, there are a number of guides to help you identify military uniforms. One of the best (and simplest) is Iain Swinnerton, *Identifying your World War I Soldier from Badges and Photographs* (Federation of Family History Societies, 2001). David J. Barnes has written a number of articles, including 'Identification and Dating of Military Uniforms' which appeared in Don Steel and Lawrence Taylor (eds), *Family History in Focus*, (Lutterworth Press, 1984). See also his 'A Brief Guide to the Identification and Dating of British Military Photographs' in *Family History Monthly* (no 65) and 'Identification and Dating British Military Uniforms' in *Family and Local History Handbook* (6th edition, Genealogical Services Directory, 2002). Illustrations of regimental badges (of varying quality) can be seen on-line at http://members.tripod.com/regtwarpath.

BADGES OF RANK AND PROFICIENCY.
N.C.O.'s AND MEN.

Regimental Quartermaster Sergeant.

Colour-Sergeant.

Scout Corporal.

Quartermaster Sergeant.

Sergeant.

Squadron Scout.

Company Sergeant-Major.

Corporal.

Bugler.

Lance-Corporal.

Colour-Sergeant, Rifle Regiments.

Infantry Pioneer.

Bugler, Rifle Regiment.

Roughrider.

Sergeant Trumpeter.

A table of Army proficiency badges.

Mr Barnes will also identify military uniforms for a small fee. He can be contacted at 148 Parkinson Street, Burnley BB11 3LL or visit www.rfc-rnas-raf-register.org.uk.

BACKGROUND READING

It is also a good idea to familiarise yourself with the period by doing some background reading. A general history of the war will help to put your research into context and provide some background to the events that your soldier or village went through. Some suggestions are given in Appendix IV. There are also hundreds of more specialised books, ranging from accounts of individual regiments or types of aircraft to detailed histories of campaigns, battles or even particular days of the war that can provide more information.

It may be difficult to track down some of the more specialist books. If you've got internet access you can find out what is currently in print by visiting the Amazon website (www.amazon.co.uk). The British Library Public Catalogue (www.blpc.bl.uk) will supply you with details of virtually every book ever published in Britain. By the end of 2003 the catalogue to the collection of printed books held by the Imperial War Museum should also be available on-line (www.iwm.org.uk). Otherwise you will need to talk to your local library staff (ideally in the reference or local studies library) to see what they can find for you.

WHERE THE RECORDS ARE

Books may not be able to answer the queries you have, or stimulate other questions, particularly if you are researching individuals or small units. This means having to look at original material, which may prove to be time-consuming (but deeply addictive and rewarding). Most original documents can be found in one of several places: a national repository or museum, a regimental or service museum, a local studies library or a county record office. In brief, records of the armed forces and the most important private papers are held at national repositories such as the National Archives (formerly the Public Record Office) and the Imperial War Museum. Regimental and service museums may have archival material relating to their regiment or service, while at local record offices and local studies libraries is material about the locality (such as local government, people and businesses). There are also a large number of specialist repositories for businesses, universities and charities, that may have information. In my time I've used the archives of the British Red Cross Society and Royal Star and Garter Home; company archives may include papers about employees who served in the forces or the provision of a memorial plaque for those who did not return.

Unfortunately, there is no hard or fast rule to who has what, so the papers of a particular commander may be with a local archive, or material about a local munitions factory could be at the National Archives. However, the Historical Manuscripts Commission runs the National Register of Archives, which lists many holdings at local record offices, some museums and specialist repositories. It is available on-line at www.hmc.gov.uk/nra or you are welcome to use their searchroom (details in Appendix I). An alternative is the Access to Archives database (www.a2a.pro.gov.uk), which lists an increasing proportion of holdings of local record offices and some more specialist archives.

The holdings of the most important national repositories and museums are described in Appendix I. Regimental and service museums are described in Terence and Shirley Wise, *A Guide to Military Museums and Other Places of Military Interest* (10th edition, Terence Wise, 2001) or on-line (regimental museums only) at www.armymuseums.org.uk.

Every county has a local record office and most towns have a local studies or history centre. Yellow Pages or the local library should be able to tell you where the nearest one is located. Their holdings are described in Janet Foster and Julia Sheppard, *British Archives: A Guide to Archive Resources in the United Kingdom* (4th edition, Palgrave Macmillan, 2001), along with the vast majority of specialist repositories – every reference library should have a copy. Less comprehensive, but more practical, is Jeremy Gibson and Pamela Peskett, *Record Offices and How to Find Them* (8th edition, Federation of Family History Societies, 2002). ARCHON (www.hmc.gov.uk/archon) provides links to most local record offices. It can be much harder, however, to track down local studies libraries, particularly ones outside your area. Those with access to the internet can find many addresses through the Familia website: www.earl.org.uk/familia, otherwise see whether your local library has a copy of the *Library Directory 1991–1992* which contains details of local studies libraries and their holdings.

FINDING WHAT YOU WANT

Each record office has a different system of managing its records, although most follow the same principles of archive administration. Documents are kept together by collection, rather than rearranged by subject as happens in a library. This can be frustrating if you are researching a topic, as you may have to search a number of sources to find what you want. A number of repositories have electronic catalogues, notably those at the National Archives, which can identify documents in a large number of places on the same subject. They are also usually available on the internet. The on-line Access to Archives (A2A) catalogue (www.a2a.pro.gov.uk) provides the same service for local record offices and some military museums. A2A is extremely easy to use, although it is by no means comprehensive. However, you are unlikely to be able to track down an individual, as the catalogues only record the item description, rather than describe the contents themselves, so you may well have to look through records from a particular regiment or battalion before you turn up a reference to your ancestor.

Many local record offices, local studies libraries and some regimental museums, however, still rely on old-fashioned card indexes arranged by subjects. There's usually a heading for the 'First World War', and perhaps others for 'memorials' or 'conscription'.

In addition, a number of record offices, particularly the National Archives, produce useful introductory leaflets on aspects of their records. They are now often available on their websites. Where there are specific leaflets which might be of use in your research they are mentioned in the text below.

UNDERTAKING RESEARCH

It is important to ring beforehand to book a seat as most archives have very cramped reading areas. The staff should be able to give you a rough idea whether they have the records you are interested in, and indeed may have something ready when you arrive. They can also tell you whether they allow the use of laptop computers and other gadgets. You should take with you a notebook, several pencils (as pens are rarely allowed into reading rooms), any notes you might have, and a pound coin for a locker (should they be provided) for your bag and coat. It is a good idea to allow plenty of time to familiarize yourself with the archive and its finding aids, particularly if you are going to make several visits. You may also want to talk through what you hope to find with the archivist or librarian on duty, as they may be able to suggest places to look and shortcuts to take.

Written sources are the basis of all historical research. Using them properly makes the best use of your time and ensures that you get all you can from the records. The best practice is to do the following:

- Note down all the references of the documents you consult, together with their descriptions, even for those items which were useless. You may need to use them again; having the references can cut the work in half.
- Read each document thoroughly, especially if you are unfamiliar with the type of record. See whether there is an index at the front or back of a volume which could help.
- Many records come in similar form. Soldiers' service papers or battalion war diaries, for example, are much the same. Once you have mastered the style they are easy to go through.
- There may be an index or other finding aid. Ask the staff.
- If you are not sure about how to use a document or about reading it, ask the staff. They are there to help!
- Note down everything of interest in pencil, together with the reference of the document, in a notebook. Try to keep your notes legible (not, of course, a problem if you are using a laptop computer).

MAKING USE OF YOUR RESEARCH

Although research is a deeply satisfying pastime in itself, you should aim to write up your study and publish it in some way, so that other people can make use of your work (think how you benefited from the research of others) and admire your perspicacity! There are three main ways of doing this:

- You may be able to persuade a local or military history society to publish your work, alternatively you can either publish the book yourself or approach a publisher to do it for you. Whatever you do, you are unlikely to make a profit.
- Submit an article to a family, local or military history journal (depending on the subject). Editors usually welcome well-written, interesting contributions. Don't make it too long: two or three thousand words maximum.

- Putting your research on the internet is an increasingly popular alternative. It is almost free and there is literally a worldwide audience waiting to read what you've written, although it is not easy to create an attractive site that people will want to come back to as it might seem at first glance (as you'll discover if you visit many of the sites suggested in Appendix V). Most internet service providers (ISPs) will display your web pages for free. It is surprisingly easy to do, even for technical novices, as there are a number of books, magazines and internet sites which can help you.

2

EVERYDAY LIFE IN THE BRITISH ARMY

❧

Most historians have divided the war into three phases, with two periods of mobility at the very beginning and end of the war, and nearly four years of relative deadlock in the trenches between October/ November 1914 and March/August 1918. This stalemate was the result of two equally matched sides proving unable to gain the upper hand. Instead both devoted resources to the horrendous doctrine of a 'war of attrition' which attempted to kill as many of the enemy as possible – the side which had fewest soldiers would lose; a doctrine that was perfected at the Battle of Verdun in 1916. Coupled with this was the fact that the technology employed was largely defensive with huge batteries of artillery pounding enemy trenches, and when offensive weapons were developed (notably the tank) they were not employed properly. There was also the minor but important matter that the commander at the rear had little or no communication with the troops in the front line during battles – wireless was only in its infancy, and communication by runner, telephone or pigeon was easily disrupted – and so they had little idea of what was happening and could not easily direct units to where they were needed in the heat of battle.

The Western Front grew and developed until it became a unique and separate world from the countries through which it ran. Its ramifications stretched far behind the trenches that we immediately associate with the war today, to the artillery lines, the billets, the supply dumps, the training grounds, the casualty clearing stations and the base hospitals and the stables. Indeed, it was possible to spend your war service without seeing an enemy soldier. However, the First World War was the last conflict in which more troops saw action than were engaged in supporting the fighting man. There was quite a lot of resentment between the infantry who had seen frontline service and the storemen, postal workers and the clerks behind the scenes. During 1918 many of these support duties were taken over by women, thus freeing men to join more active units.

Flemish and French civilians could be found here as well, running the *estaminets* (bars), cafes and the unofficial brothels. And until 1917, when they were finally removed, many peasants continued to farm their fields close to the front line, ignoring the mayhem which was happening all around them.

This was also the first war in which the vast majority of casualties resulted from wounds rather than sickness, something which had long been a feature of British Army campaigns in the past. This was in part because of the rigorous hygienic practices enforced by the authorities which cut down on diseases such as typhoid and dysentery, but was also due to the efficient medical services. Considerable effort had gone into improving the medical services following the shambles of the Boer War. Depending on the seriousness of the wound, men were efficiently ferried back through a series of casualty clearing stations to base hospitals and where necessary to a network of hospitals in country houses and local infirmaries back in Blighty (Britain). Hundreds of thousands of men owed their lives to the dedicated doctors and nursing staff as well as to the system itself.

The men who served in the British Army during the war were almost exactly split between volunteers and conscripts. Recruits were required to be between the ages of 19 and 35, to be at least 5 feet 6 inches tall and to have a chest measurement of 34 inches. The height was quickly reduced to 5 feet 3 inches in October 1914, when the numbers volunteering began to drop. In addition, a number of Bantam Battalions of smaller men were formed.

Kitchener's call for 200,000 men in the first month resulted in 300,000 men coming forward to enlist. All in all about 2.5 million men volunteered for military service up until the end of 1915, of whom nearly a third joined in the first eight weeks of the war. Numbers soon fell away, and the authorities had to resort to increasingly desperate measures to keep the numbers up.

Conscription commenced in March 1916, after various voluntary schemes had failed to produce the required numbers. Initially only unmarried men were called to the colours, however in May 1916 the scheme was extended to married men between the ages of 18 and 41.

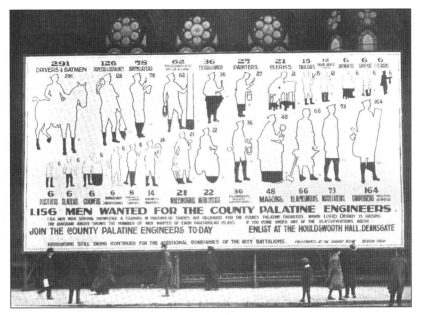

Recruiting poster outside Manchester Town Hall for a territorial battalion of the Royal Engineers. After the initial enthusiasm recruiting for the armed forces became more and more difficult.

For political reasons Ireland was excluded. In 1918 the government received powers to raise the age of conscription to 56, but the higher age was never introduced. Men working in key trades, such as miners and steelworkers, were exempt from conscription. Even so, as the war progressed, even these trades were 'combed through' (in the contemporary phrase) and non-essential men called up. Their work was increasingly undertaken by women. It was possible to appeal against the call-up on grounds of conscience (although few did) or for personal or employment reasons. This is discussed in more detail in chapters 3 and 6.

Whether conscript or volunteer, a man's first experience of the services would be the training camp, which was a period of induction into the very different world of the army, something which few civilians knew anything about. In addition there was the adjustment to living and working with many men of very different social backgrounds: particularly difficult in the socially stratified world of Edwardian England. The purpose of training was to turn the recruit into an

24

Recruits in the Scots Guards training at Caterham. Training raw recruits to obey without hesitation was regarded as being of immense importance by the Army.

unthinking automaton who would obey an order without question. This was done by rigorous drilling that was largely unchanged since Napoleonic times. Much attention, for example, was devoted to the bayonet, even though it was virtually useless on the battlefield. The result was to produce men in whom initiative and imagination had virtually been destroyed. This made for good cannon fodder, but the conditions of war so often demanded men to react quickly and imaginatively to conditions on the ground. Colonial troops, particularly the Australians, were not treated in the same way. Although British staff officers protested at their indiscipline and unwillingness to salute officers, they had to admire their fighting ability and bravery.

One aspect of training was to build both a close link with immediate comrades and an intense pride in the regiment in which one served, which was encouraged by lectures in the regimental tradition and its glorious history and the fostering of the little differences between it and other units. From the 1880s most infantry regiments were linked to a particular county or district and recruited most of their soldiers from there. This link was broken in the latter part of the war, partly because of the devastating effect that the destruction of the Pals battalions (units recruited from a particular area or occupation) during the Battle of the Somme had on towns such as Accrington, but mainly because the operational needs meant transferring drafts of men from one regiment to another. This was often met with surprising resentment among ordinary soldiers. However, this territorial link was not always certain: there were a surprising proportion of men from Norfolk in Highland regiments because several battalions were recruiting in the county as war broke out.

Eventually training would be completed and the men sent to France. Those with specialist skills would be sent to specialist units – railwaymen, for example, to Royal Engineer Railway Sections, which were responsible for running and maintaining the network of light railways that criss-crossed the Western Front. Ordinary infantrymen most likely would go for further training at one of the large bases, where some attempt was made to instil the basics required to survive a spell in the trenches. The largest of these was at Etaples, just south of

81.   THE KING AT THE FRONT.   "The smile of Victory"—

HM King George V (centre) with Sir Douglas Haig (right) and French commanders during a visit to France in 1917. (Joe Pie Picture Library)

Boulogne, where conditions and the discipline were appalling. So bad, indeed, that it was here that the only serious British mutiny of the war took place in 1917.

Eventually the battalion would be sent up the line. Slow moving trains would take troops part of the way. Then at the railhead the battalion would line up and march towards the front. It was something that soldiers became all too familiar with: fifty minutes marching about three miles, followed by ten minutes' rest. On each man's back would be a pack containing all his possessions (including clothing and family photographs), his rifle, one hundred rounds of ammunition, trench tools, water and rations. It weighed some 55lb and for smaller men and the tired it was a real burden.

In contrast, officers' baggage, and usually that of their servants (or batmen), was carried in one of the regimental trucks. Lives of officers were, in general, much easier and indeed, except in the front line they lived almost totally separated from their men. Officers were expected to equip themselves at their own expense in the military equivalent of hunting dress, with riding boots and breeches and a Sam Browne belt. They were assigned a batman to look after their personal possessions. The food was better, leave was more generous and the best restaurants in the towns behind the frontline were reserved for officers. The Toc H Club, run by Tubby Clayton in Poperinghe, was almost unique when it told guests to leave their rank at the door and treated everybody the same.

Proportionally, however, casualties were much higher, particularly for junior officers (second lieutenants and lieutenants) who led their platoons and sections on raids and over the top into battle. Initially, officers came from the public schools as they always had, but the demands of war meant that this was increasingly not sufficient. By 1916 a growing proportion of officers had been promoted from the ranks. Before the war perhaps a dozen officers each year were selected in this way. Officers could now be sons of miners or land agents, salesmen or students – 'temporary gentlemen' in the eyes of many senior officers and the press – who sometimes had great difficulty in fitting in with what was expected of them socially. Often, however, working and middle class replacements proved themselves just as good as their public schooled predecessors and soon acquired the same mannerisms. Once selected, officers attended an initial training course. In 1914 this lasted just a month and finished with a soccer or rugby game where men were judged by the suitable speed and grit they displayed. By late 1915 the course had become more professional and lasted three months, before the new officers were sent back to the front.

The Western Front did not comprise of just a single long trench, but a complex and often confusing maze of lines and connecting paths. The front-line system was made up of three parallel lines – the fire trench facing the enemy, the travel trench at 20 yards, and further back the support line, close enough to reinforce in case of a raid. All three lines were built in a zig-zag shape with bays every couple of yards, separated by sharp turns in the line designed to minimise bomb-blast and to easily contain a German raiding party should one get into the trench. Trenches were about four feet deep, with a built-up wall of sandbags as a parapet to allow men to stand upright. Along the floor ran a drainage tunnel covered by duckboards (lengths of wooden ladders). Facing the enemy was the firestep on which men stood while on sentry duty or before an attack was launched. Dug into no-man's-land were small lengths of trench known as saps, again occupied by sentries, machine gunners or used by raiding parties. In the support line could be found officers' dugouts (warm and comfortable caves dug deep below the trench) together with kitchens, latrines (toilets), stores and mortar positions.

Most soldiers spent relatively short periods at the front – 48 or 72 hours were not uncommon. To an extent this depended on whether troops were being sent to a quiet part of the line or not. But this excluded the time spent marching to and from the front line area and then inching their way through the maze of support trenches, with the intention of arriving at twilight. It was not uncommon for parties to get lost as they struggled forward. The new arrival was amazed by what he found. Richard Mottram later described his first experience of the front line:

> Enormous noise. Continuous explosions. A deserted landscape, complete immobility of everything. Men were eating, smoking, doing odd jobs, but no one was fighting. A few were peering in periscopes or looking through loopholes. I tried but could see nothing but upturned empty fields. Then suddenly there was a terrific crash which flung me yards. I picked myself up and did my best to laugh. Nearby a man lay with a tiny hole in his forehead and close to him another limped away with blood pumping out of his leg. They were both carried away. A casualty was not a matter for horror, but replacement.

Men would prepare carefully for their time at the front. With their packs left behind, haversacks would be stuffed with chocolate, candle ends, and cigarettes in every pocket or cranny. If the weather was cold, sheepskins, cardigans and fingerless leather gloves jostled for place with periscopes, bolt cutters, sandbags and other material for trench stores. The men looked like explorers to a remote part of the world – as indeed they were.

Most soldiers found trench life a greater strain than battle, for it was strain unrelieved by excitement. Training had not prepared men for this vigilant inaction, let alone for their seeing colleagues and friends killed or wounded.

Once the men had arrived and become accustomed to their new surroundings, then they would be introduced to an inflexible timetable. Day started with stand-to half an hour before daybreak, when all men waited with rifles on the firestep, because it was thought this was the time at which the enemy was most likely to attack. After dawn, leaving sentries in post, most men filed off for breakfast. The day would be

Scroll of honour issued to men discharged from the Army at the end of the war.

spent in a mixture of odd-jobs (perhaps repairing damaged sandbags, carrying ammunition or resetting loose duckboards), sentry duty, or resting. At dusk there would be a flurry of activity as new parties of troops as well as the rations arrived.

Night was the most active and most dangerous time. Raiding parties, always made up of volunteers, were sent into no-man's-land to repair damaged barbed wire or to try to find out what the enemy was up to. Pockets were emptied, faces blackened with burnt cork and bayonets dulled with a covering sock, before scrambling over the top, hoping to avoid machine gun fire, and crawling through the wire. The Germans were engaged in the same activities, so a lot of time was spent avoiding them: one veteran thought it was like a game of poachers and gamekeepers.

Everyday life was made worse by the weather, particularly in low-lying Belgium where shelling had destroyed the drainage system. Except in the very driest months, water and mud were to be found everywhere. The trenches were infested by rats, some of which grew to enormous size and seemed fearless of man. The men themselves were often covered by lice and much time was spent finding and killing them, although in general to little effect. The verb *to chat*, which originally meant to kill lice, took on a more pleasant definition during the war. For most men the compensation was the development of a close comradeship with their fellow soldiers; it was one of the few things which was missed when they returned to civilian life. This companionship was also influential in ensuring that morale and discipline was maintained, and may explain why so many gallantry medals were won for rescuing wounded comrades.

The amount of fighting a man saw during his time in the trenches depended very much on the sector to which he was assigned. In many places, what became known as the 'live and let live system' developed, where both sides operated what was in effect nearly an unofficial truce, engaging in the bare minimum of warfare sufficient to keep their generals happy. In other places, however, there could be continual bombardments, night raids and general harassment of the enemy.

The war, of course, is known for its long and very bloody battles, notably Ypres in 1915, the Somme in 1916 and Passchendaele in 1917, which saw the deaths of many hundreds of thousands of men in the mud and confusion which resulted. In each case very similar tactics were involved. A week or more of heavy bombardment would, it was claimed, have destroyed German positions and demoralised the enemy troops. This would be followed by waves of infantry scrambling into no-man's-land and advancing slowly behind artillery fire to take the enemy line. Indeed when the strategy worked, as it did on occasion, it could see rapid advances. However, more often the enemy dugouts were not destroyed and the advancing troops were met with a deadly hail of fire from German machine guns, which killed and wounded many men, but disorientated and frightened others who sought refuge in shell-holes. And as there were virtually no communications sent back from the fighting the artillery had little idea of where the advance had reached, so couldn't support the infantry as efficiently as they would have wished. More importantly, the generals commanding had little idea of the situation on the ground and were inclined to believe the most optimistic of intelligence reports, which is one reason why the battles always lasted for many weeks longer than they should have. Only in 1918, when the bloody lessons had at last been learnt and effective use was made of tanks and aircraft, did the position change.

In general, ordinary soldiers received little home leave, perhaps a

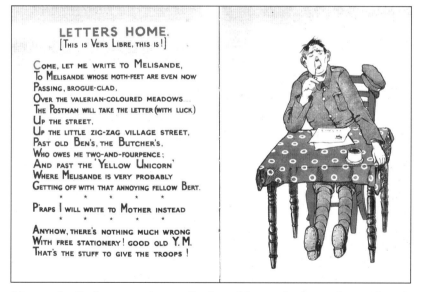

Many a family has a precious collection of letters from men 'somewhere in France'. The YM in this poem is the YMCA who, during the war, supplied many hundreds of thousands of sheets of writing paper to enable soldiers to write home. (Joe Pie Picture Library)

week a year, although the provision of leave was much more generous for officers. Instead the few precious leisure hours (and the Army liked to occupy every moment of soldiers' lives) were spent in the YMCA and other recreational huts provided by the Army itself and other charities. A preferred alternative was to visit the local *estaminets* or cafes, to enjoy a plate of egg and chips (the soldiers' favourite meal), drink a few glasses of rough wine ('plonk' as it became known) and perhaps flirt with the owner and her daughters. Here the war and its horrors could be forgotten for a few short hours.

Not everyone, of course, returned to enjoy their egg and chips. Junior officers were particularly likely to die in battle; a quarter of officers were killed in action, compared with an eighth of other ranks. Few frontline troops would escape from being wounded at some stage. A sample of 48,000 admissions to casualty clearing stations showed that just 21% of men were hit in the body, with 51% in the arms and legs and 17% in the head. The numbers of men affected by shellshock (the medical term used was neurasthenia), stress or other psychological traumas is not recorded. The most prized wound was a 'blighty one', that is, an injury that was not fatal but was serious enough for the

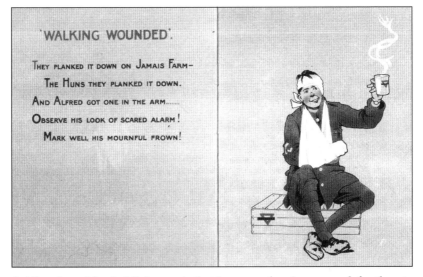

Soldiers hoped for 'a blighty one', that is a wound serious enough for them to be sent back to Britain but not one which left a permanent disability. (Joe Pie Picture Library)

patient to have to return to Britain for treatment. Despite the inevitable errors, the care and attention offered the wounded was very high. It might take a day to get a seriously injured man from the front line to a base hospital on the French coast and a couple of days more to a hospital back in England.

After the Armistice in November 1918, the army rapidly began to demobilise. Within a year, what had been the largest army in the world was reduced to little more than its pre-war size. Few men were unchanged by their experiences in the forces. The unlucky ones were mentally and physically scarred for life. Even apparently normal men might suffer horrendous nightmares as they relived time and again the horrors of the trenches. A surprising number, though, enjoyed their time in the forces as a chance to escape from a humdrum job and develop new skills that otherwise they would never have had the chance to learn. Most men remembered the friendships that developed under fire and in battle against a common enemy, whether it be the Germans or the British High Command.

3

TRACING INDIVIDUAL SOLDIERS

❦

The vast majority of British men who fought during the First World War served in the Army. Just over half saw action at the front. The others were engaged in supporting roles from cooking meals to charting maps, undoubtedly important work but undeniably less romantic.

The Army was divided between officers, who received a commission from the King, non-commissioned officers (sergeants and corporals) and the ordinary soldier, or 'tommy' as he was often nicknamed by the press. Officers tended to come from the middle and upper classes. By 1917 however, as casualties mounted, their numbers were diluted by men from the lower middle class and even the working class.

One of the features of the early years of the war was the creation of 'pals battalions', when men from a particular town or occupation enlisted together. This undoubtedly helped recruiting and boosted local patriotism, but the cruel downside was that a particular district could be devastated after a battle. The best known example of this was the small Lancashire mill town of Accrington, which suffered badly after the local Pals Battalion (11th Service Battalion, East Lancashire Regiment) was torn apart at the Battle of Serre on 1 July 1916: out of a total of 720 men, just 136 returned. For more information about the Accrington Pals visit www.btinternet.com/ ~a.Jackson. A series of books about individual pals battalions have been published by Leo Cooper (for details of the publisher see Appendix IV).

SERVICE RECORDS

OFFICERS

Officers are listed in the *Army Lists*, which were published quarterly during the war. For intelligence reasons the information given is not as comprehensive as would be found in peacetime lists. Even so it should be possible to track down promotions and the date they were made. The National Archives has a complete set on the shelves in the Microfilm Reading Room, and copies can be found elsewhere. Officers also appear in the medal index cards which are described in more detail below.

Some 85% of officers' service records are at Kew. However, if your ancestor left the service after April 1922, or rejoined during the Second World War, then his record is still with the Ministry of Defence. In addition, records of Guards officers are with the regimental record offices (for addresses see below).

At some stage the records were sorted out and much material was destroyed. What survives tends to be correspondence concerning money, length of service and pensions, rather than about an individual's war service. Even so these documents are still of great interest. There are, in fact, several series of records in series WO 339 (with an index in WO 338) and WO 374. With the exception of WO 338, the documents have not been microfilmed. WO 374 consists of files of Territorial Army officers, officers who came out of retirement, and other officers recruited because of their skills in civilian life (such as railway managers). This series is arranged in alphabetical order, so is easy to use. Service files for a few notable individuals, including Field Marshal Lord Haig and the poet Wilfred Owen, are in WO 138.

Biographical details of officers in the Army Medical Corps are listed in Sir William Macarlane's *A List of Commissioned Medical Officers of the Army, 1660–1960* (Wellcome Library, 1968). Both the National Archives' and Society of Genealogists' libraries have copies. There are also a number of rolls of honour listing officers who had fallen – these are listed below.

OTHER RANKS

Service records for non-commissioned officers (NCOs) and ordinary soldiers who served in the British Army between August 1914 and the end of 1920 can be very informative. They can tell you when a man enlisted and was discharged, who his next of kin was, and give details of promotions through the ranks and units served in, as well as medical treatment received and appearances before courts martial. There may also be correspondence about pension or medal claims or, in at least one case, the medical chart on his hospital bed showing the man's

Symbols of officers' ranks.

36

temperature before an operation. What the records will not do is to tell you very much about any fighting he was engaged in. However, you can use the war diaries to obtain this information (see below).

These records can only be seen at the National Archives. They are arranged in strict alphabetical order by surname and then by forenames. It obviously helps that you know in which unit a man served and his regimental number, particularly for men with common names. There are thousands of files for John Smith and John Jones, for example, so which one was yours? There are also a small number of miscellaneous files, found during filming the documents, at the end of the series.

Unfortunately, records survive for only about a third of men, although as will be seen there are other sources to build up a rough idea of a man's army service for those of us whose ancestor's service records have been lost. In general it can be said that if your ancestor was killed in action, there is less likely to be a file for him – perhaps a one in four or one in five chance. The vast majority were lost during a fire in September 1940. In addition, these records do not include those for men who served in the Household Cavalry or the Guards regiments, which are kept separately.

There are several series that you may need to consult:

WO 363	known as the 'burnt' records, as they were damaged in some way by fire or water in 1940. The originals were in very fragile condition, which is why the decision was taken to film them. They are for men who were killed in action, died of wounds or disease without being discharged to service, or demobilised at the end of the war.
WO 364	known as the 'unburnt' records, because they were either untouched by the fire or subsequently added to from other sources. They are generally for men who were either regular soldiers before the war and who were discharged at the end of their service, or men who later claimed disability pensions.
WO 400	Service records for men of the Household Cavalry, which included the Life Guards, Royal Horse Guards, and Household Battalions. These records are complete.

Records of soldiers and non-commissioned officers discharged from the five Footguards Regiments (Grenadiers, Coldstream, Scots, Irish,

Welsh) are in the custody of their respective Regimental Headquarters at Wellington Barracks, Birdcage Walk, London SW1E 6HQ. Again these records are complete.

More information about these records can be found in a free leaflet: *British Army Soldiers' Papers: First World War, 1914–1918* (Military Records Information 9), which can be downloaded from the National Archives website (www.pro.gov.uk) or ordered by ringing their help line on 020 8392 5200.

If your ancestor continued to serve in the Army after the end of 1920, his service record will be with the Ministry of Defence, Army Personnel Centre, Historic Disclosures, Mailpoint 400, Kentigern House, 65 Brown St, Glasgow G2 8EX, tel 0141 224 2023, e-mail apcsec@dial.pipex.com.

CASUALTIES

The dead of the First World War are recorded in many ways, all of which can provide useful information about an ancestor who sacrificed his life for the greater good.

COMMONWEALTH WAR GRAVES COMMISSION

The Commonwealth War Graves Commission was set up to commemorate the dead of the First World War and has done its best to find and record as many war deaths of British and Commonwealth men as possible from 1914. It is perhaps best known for the hundreds of carefully tended, and very moving, cemeteries scattered through northern France and Belgium. Their database, known as the Debt of Honour roll, is on-line at www.cwgc.org and it will tell you where a man is buried, when he died, his rank and the unit with which he served. They also provide the same information to people who write in or telephone their offices; (address is given in Appendix I). Another website, www.cwgc.co.uk, is devoted to errors and omissions in the CWGC Debt of Honour roll.

SOLDIERS DIED

For the First World War the deaths of 37,000 officers and 635,000 soldiers are recorded in *Soldiers Died in the Great War*. Originally this was a multi-volume book, but it is now available on CD-ROM, which

A visitor inspects the British memorial at Menin Gate, Ypres, which records the names of the 55,000 men who lost their lives at the Ypres Salient. Memorials like this bring home the human cost of the war far better than any statistics could.

makes it very easy to search. The information contained about individuals varies and is by no means accurate, but will indicate where a man died, his rank and the regiment he was with. It may also tell you where and when a man enlisted and his age at enlistment. Virtually every reference library or family history society library worth its salt should have a copy of the CD, and copies can be bought from Naval and Military Press (address in Appendix IV).

WAR MEMORIALS

After the war some 45,000 war memorials were erected in honour of men who did not return, usually for a locality or regiment or other unit and sometimes for schools, churches or work places (I recently came across one dedicated to the milkmen of the Thames Valley). They take a variety of forms – the most common is a memorial cross, but they vary from playing fields to hospital beds. An ancestor's name may appear on two or three such memorials, or in rare cases may have been missed off altogether. Normally all you will find is his name, though sometimes the rank and unit and details of gallantry medals will also be included. In small villages everybody who served in the forces may be listed, not just the deceased.

There is no list of who appears on which memorial. However, the UK National Inventory of War Memorials based at the Imperial War Museum, is identifying and preparing a database of memorials for all wars. At present, the database can only be used in the reading room at the IWM, but it will eventually be made available on-line. Their records sometimes include transcriptions of the names on the memorials, but this is by no means universal. More about the Inventory and its work can be found at www.iwm.org.uk/collections/niwm/index.htm or by contacting the Museum itself (address in Appendix I).

There are a surprising number of websites on war memorials and the men who appear on them. Most are listed in Stuart A. Raymond, *War Memorials on the Web* (2 parts, Federation of Family History Societies, 2003). One of the best sites of this kind, about Cheltenham, can be found at www.remembering.org.uk.

A number of studies about the men who appear on local war memorials have been researched in recent years. It is worth asking in your local library to see whether one has been done for your area.

ROLLS OF HONOUR

Several national rolls of honour have been published with details of officers who died during the war. Entries for some 25,000 officers (including 7,000 photographs) were collected and published in 1917 by the Marquis Melville de Ruvigny, a noted genealogist of the period: *De Ruvigny's Roll of Honour: A Biographical Record of His Majesty's Military and Aerial Forces Who Fell in the Great War 1914–1917*. It has been reprinted by the London Stamp Exchange (1987) and the Military and Naval Press (2001). More recently S.B. and D.B. Jarvis, *The Cross of Sacrifice: Officers Who Died in the Service of the British, Indian and East African Regiments and Corps, 1914–1919* (Naval and Military Press, 1993) combines the information in the Debt of Honour Roll and *Soldiers Died* in alphabetical order.

In the years after the war many companies and schools prepared rolls of honour listing employees or ex-students who served or perhaps just those who had fallen. On occasion short personal biographies may be included. A probably incomplete list is given in Norman Holding's *The Location of British Army Records 1914–1918*. At the National Archives, for example, lists of employees of the Midland Railway who were either wounded or killed in action are in RAIL 491/1259. A similar roll of honour for men of the London, Brighton and South Coast Railway is in RAIL 414/761 and for the North Eastern Railway in RAIL 527/993. Some rolls for schools are with the Society of Genealogists. The Naval and Military Press has reprinted a number of such rolls.

Again, a fair number of rolls of honour appear on-line. Links to a number of such sites can be found at www.roll-of-honour.com. For example, a fully searchable roll of honour to many of the Suffolk men who made the ultimate sacrifice can be found at www.suffolkcc.gov.uk/sro/roh.

OTHER CASUALTY RECORDS

French and Belgian death certificates for British soldiers who died in hospitals or elsewhere outside the immediate war zone between 1914 and 1920 are in RG 35/45-69. They are arranged by first letter of surname.

Newspapers, local as well as national, published casualty lists. In addition, most local newspapers included short biographies of men from the district who lost their lives, sometimes with a photograph. Increasing shortages of paper meant that this practice was curtailed from mid-1917 onwards.

It is possible to get ordinary death certificates for servicemen from the General Register Office, or in person at the Family Records Centre. For details see Appendix I.

HOSPITAL RECORDS

An efficient system was quickly introduced on the outbreak of war to ferry the sick and wounded to the appropriate casualty clearing station or hospital in the rear. A record card was compiled for each man, but all these records (with the exception of a 2% sample) were destroyed in the early 1980s, before their value for family historians and academic researchers was realised. The surviving cards are in series MH 106. The records of the hospitals themselves too have largely been destroyed. Again, a small number of examples can be found in MH 106. If the hospital in Britain to which an ancestor was sent had been a pre-war charity or public hospital, rather than one established in a country house for the duration of the war, it might be worth checking the Wellcome Institute/National Archives on-line database of hospital records (http://hospitalrecords.pro.gov.uk) to see whether anything survives. The medical system and the records it created are described in more detail in Norman Holding, *More Sources of World War I Army Ancestry.*

An interesting website devoted to the pioneering work of Queen Mary's Hospital, Sidcup, in plastic surgery during the war can be found at http://website.lineone.net/~andrewwbamji/index.htm.

The most famous hospital opened during the war was the Star and Garter Home which began caring for a few of the most badly injured soldiers, sailors and airmen in 1916. The hospital began life in an old hotel on the top of Richmond Hill in south-west London. The most useful records are patients' registers recording a man's unit, where he was transferred from, the reason for admission and his fate, normally death, but often in the early days for insurbordination. They are retained by the Home and can be consulted by appointment, by contacting the Archivist, Royal Star and Garter Home, Richmond TW10 6RR, www.starandgarter.org.

PENSION RΔECORDS

Widows and disabled ex-servicemen were entitled to claim a pension. Much ill-feeling was created by the low level of the pension and the difficulties placed in the way of claimants by the government and local officials supervising the grant of awards. Detailed records were naturally kept, but most were destroyed in the early 1980s because the Public Record Office did not think they were of any interest. The protests caused by this wanton act of vandalism ensured that when it came to decide the fate of the service records they did not suffer the same fate. However, PIN 82 contains an 8% sample of widows' and dependents' papers for all services arranged in alphabetical order. Another sample of pensions awarded in the London area is in PIN 26. It may also be worth looking at the registered files of the Ministry of Pensions in PIN 15. There are several series of records relating to wartime claims made by officers and their families in PMG 42-PMG 47.

PRISONERS OF WAR

Nearly 200,000 British and Commonwealth prisoners of war fell into the hands of the Germans and their allies during the war, about half of whom were captured during the last six months of the war. Conditions could be grim, in part because of deliberate mistreatment, but more often because of increasing problems within Germany itself. Many prisoners eventually depended largely on Red Cross parcels, which were collected and packed by voluntary organisations under the leadership of the British Red Cross.

Unfortunately, it is difficult to find out very much about individual POWs, largely because detailed Red Cross registers and other records were lost in the late 1920s. A list of prisoners in German and Turkish hands in 1916 can be found at the National Archives in AIR 1/892/204/5/696-698, which indicates where the prisoner was captured and when, where he was held and his next of kin. There is a published *List of Officers taken Prisoner in the Various Theatres of War between August 1914 and November 1918* (1919, reprinted London Stamp Exchange, 1988). Copies are in the National Archives' and Society of Genealogists' libraries. Returning British prisoners were interrogated by the authorities about their experiences and a selection of these reports (with an index) is in series WO 161. Reports by officers may be found in their service records (see above). There are occasional mentions of individual prisoners and their conditions in the correspondence of the Foreign Office Prisoner of War Department (FO 383), although the Department was largely responsible for civilian prisoners. There is a card index to these records in the Research Enquiries Room, and if you are interested in the topic of prisoners of war in the First World War it is worth asking for the unpublished guide by Alan Bowgen called *Researching British and Commonwealth POWs of the First World War.*

Some records can also be found at the Imperial War Museum. The Women's War Work Collection, for example, contains many postcards from prisoners acknowledging the receipt of Red Cross parcels as well as correspondence from the various charities involved in the provision of these parcels.

The International Committee of the Red Cross (ICRC) in Geneva was responsible for passing details of prisoners of war between the various combatant nations and ensuring that conditions in the camps were adequate. Voluminous records were maintained which are closed for 100 years, however their archivists will search the records for you. You need to contact the ICRC Archives, 19 avenue de la Paix, CH-1202 Genève, Switzerland. More information can be found at www.icrc.org.

More about the experience of POWs can found in Richard van Emden, *Prisoners of the Kaiser: the last POWs of the Great War* (Pen and Sword, 2000) and Robert Jackson, *The Prisoners 1914–1918* (Routledge, 1989).

OPERATIONAL RECORDS

WAR DIARIES

Army units of battalion size, or larger, on active service were required to keep a daily record of all significant events together with other information such as details of operations, casualties and maps. War diaries exist for British, Dominion, Indian and Colonial forces, mainly in France and Flanders, Italy, Gallipoli, Mesopotamia, Palestine, Salonika and Russia, but rarely for units stationed in the British Isles.

They are mainly found in series WO 95 and are one of the most important sources for tracing an officer or other rank, as service papers rarely give detailed information about an individual's day-to-day life in the Army. The amount of detail in the diaries varies greatly and may depend on the enthusiasm of the responsible officer and the circumstances in which they were completed. During the heat of battle the battalion adjutant often had better things to do than keep the war diary up to date. The diary for the 1st Battalion, Hampshire Regiment, which lost 26 officers and 559 soldiers on 1st July 1916, just contains the following entry: 'The casualties of officers amounted to 100% and was also heavy in the other ranks'.

It is unusual for individuals, particularly ordinary soldiers, to be mentioned by name. Normally it is only officers who appear, most commonly when they were wounded (or killed) or undertook an unusual operation. However, the lack of personal names is not necessarily important: knowing that your ancestor was in that unit is sufficient to build up a picture of what he was engaged in.

It can be difficult to track down individual war diaries as the class list was arranged by formation rather than by unit. At the front of the list is an index showing to which higher formations infantry battalion and other units were assigned. If you have difficulty finding the unit you require (and this is not unusual), then staff will help you to locate the correct references. A few extracts from the diaries that contained secret or confidential information are now available in WO 154. Many of the maps, which were originally included in the diaries, have been extracted and added to WO 153.

TRENCH MAPS

Both sides maintained extremely complex systems of trenches, which stretched for hundreds of kilometres along the Western Front. Detailed maps were prepared for use in planning and the operations themselves. The particular emphasis of British cartographers was the German lines (which appear in red) rather than the Allied side (in blue) – indeed, it is unusual to find a map with British trenches marked. Many maps are very detailed, although it has to be said that they are difficult to use unless you are an experienced map reader or an enthusiastic student of the war itself. A few examples, from 1917 around Ypres, can be found at www.worldwar1.com/maptr01.htm.

Collections of maps are held by both the National Archives and the Imperial War Museum. Local regimental museums and other archives may also have smaller collections. More about how to use them appears at www.1914-1918.net/trench_maps.htm, and the National Archives also has a leaflet which can be consulted in the Map and Large Document Reading Room at Kew.

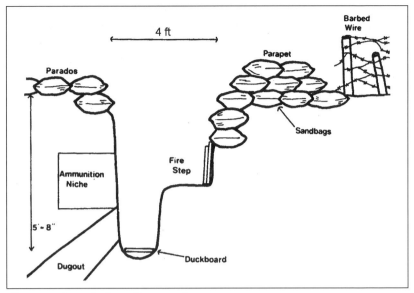

Cross-section of a front-line trench.

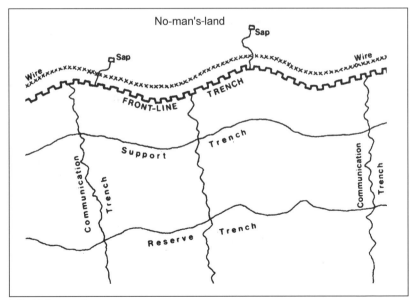

A British trench system.

Naval and Military Press has published several CD-ROMs containing examples of trench-mapping. For more information about these CDs visit www.smithmaps.fsnet.co.uk/indexmap.htm. In addition, some facsimiles have been published by G. H. Smith and Son, Easingwold, York YO6 3AB (www.ghsmith.com/worldwar1/trenchmaps.html), which can be bought directly from the company or via the Western Front Association and other outlets.

PHOTOGRAPHS AND FILM

Although the National Archives has a small number of photographs (particularly aerial shots in WO 316), the largest collection is at the Imperial War Museum. At the heart of the Museum's collections are the 40,000 official photographs taken by British and Empire photographers. As it took some time for a satisfactory system to be set up, and to overcome suspicion from the military authorities, the photographic record is more from mid-1916 onwards than for the first half of the war. This collection is supplemented by material donated by individual servicemen. The IWM's Photographic Archive, however, is not able to tell you whether they have any pictures of your ancestor. They welcome visitors to go through the photographic collections for themselves, although you should contact the Archive in advance. Regimental museums and local studies libraries may also have collections of material.

The postal address for the IWM Photographic Archive can be found in Appendix I. The Archive's reading room, however, is in the All Saints Annexe, Austral St, London SE11 – a few minutes walk from the Museum itself. The telephone number is 020 7416 5333.

The Imperial War Museum also has by far the largest collection of films for the period. Its collection is described in Roger Smithers (ed), *The Imperial War Museum Film Catalogue Volume 1: The First World War* (Flick Books, 1997). The best-known film of the period is *The Battle of the Somme*, which was eventually seen by two-thirds of the British population when it was first released in late 1916. It is now available on video and it is worth getting hold of a copy as it offers a unique picture of the British Army on the Western Front. To use the Film and Video Archive, you will need to make an appointment. They can also copy material to VHS for you to view at home. Like the Photographic Archive, they are based in the All Saints Annexe. Their phone number is 020 7416 5291. There are also a number of regional

The reading room at the Imperial War Museum where you can peruse many personal papers relating to the First World War. (Imperial War Museum)

film archives, which may have film of the period. The largest of these is the North West Film and Video Archive in Manchester. For more about using film archives in family history see issue 82 of *Family History Monthly*. A few newsreels from the period can be downloaded (for free) from www.britishpathe.com.

ORDERS OF BATTLE

It can sometimes be helpful to know in which division or corps a battalion or artillery battery was serving and perhaps where it was based. There are several ways of finding this out. Monthly Orders of Battle record the movements of units and their transfers between higher formations. Copies can be found in WO 95/5467-5481 and WO 153. However, for most purposes, the indexes which are found at the beginning of the class list for WO 95 will suffice. There are also several websites that contain similar informtion: http//members.tripod.com/ regtwarpath/index.htm and the more detailed www.orbat.com (to which you have to subscribe for certain orders).

MEDALS AND AWARDS

CAMPAIGN MEDALS

Every serviceman and woman (as well as a few civilians) who saw service overseas was entitled to two campaign medals, the British War Medal and the Victory Medal. In addition, men who had seen service in France and Flanders between 5 August and 22 November 1914 were awarded the 1914 Star (often called 'The Mons Star') and those who served overseas between 5 August 1914 and 31 December 1915 were entitled to the 1914/15 Star. Two other campaign medals were also awarded to soldiers – the Territorial Forces War Medal (awarded to members of the Territorial Forces at the beginning of the war who saw service overseas) and the Silver War Badge (for men who were discharged because of wounds or sickness).

Details of the people to whom these medals were awarded are recorded on Medal Index Cards in the Microfilm Reading Room at the National Archives. These cards cover both the Army and the Royal Air Force. The alphabetical sequence within each surname can be slightly confusing: all those with a single forename (or initial) come first; these are followed by all those with two forenames, and then by those who have three. However, as you may not know of the existence of a second or third name, or the second or third name was not used, you need to be careful.

The great advantage with these cards is that they list everyone who was entitled to a medal, which is doubly helpful if the Army service record you are looking for has been destroyed. In particular they can tell you: rank, regimental number, unit served in, other medals awarded, date of discharge, the theatre of war in which he served, and the date he was sent overseas. There are often other references, particularly to the despatch of medals to widows and next of kin of men killed in action, but it is now often difficult to decipher what these meant.

Using these cards it is possible to track the individual in the medal rolls themselves in WO 329, but as the information is almost identical, with the exception of the silver war badge, it probably isn't worth the effort.

GALLANTRY MEDALS

Gallantry medals were awarded for acts of heroism and bravery on the field of battle. In most cases it is not possible to find out very much about why a medal was awarded, as citations were rarely published. Sometimes medals were given out almost randomly to members of a platoon or company, which had seen action. As men in the front line said, 'they had come up with the rations'.

Details of all awards were published in the *London Gazette*, sometimes with a citation or short description of why the medal was awarded. At the very least you will get the man's name, service number, rank, regiment and the date when the award was made. The National Archives has copies (in series ZJ 1) together with indexes in the Microfilm Reading Room. The *Gazette* may also be found in other libraries. Digitised copies are now available on-line at www.gazettes-online.co.uk. The website is fully indexed. For awards of the Military Medal (MM) and Meritorious Service Medal (MSM) this is the only information you are likely to find.

More about medals (both gallantry and campaign) can be found in William Spencer, *Army Service Records of the First World War*.

The most common award was the Mention in Despatches (MiD). During the war just over 2% of the men in the British forces (141,082 officers and other ranks) were so honoured. At the time the only reward was a mention in the *London Gazette*, but subsequently King George V authorised the issue of a commemorative letter to holders and men were entitled to wear a stylised bronze oak leaf on their uniforms.

The most famous gallantry medal is of course the Victoria Cross. Biographies of many of the 633 award-winners, together with descriptions of their exploits, are included in an excellent series of books by Gerald Gliddon (and other authors) which have been published by Sutton Publishing over the past five years or so. There are also several websites devoted to VC winners, of which www.chapter-one.com/vc is the probably the most comprehensive. A register of VC winners can be found in series WO 98, together with copies of citations and other information.

The Distinguished Service Order (DSO) was normally only awarded to senior officers, while the Military Cross (MC) was awarded for acts of bravery to officers of the rank of captain or below. A register, arranged by the date the awards appeared in the *London Gazette*, is in WO 390 at the National Archives, while annotated copies of the *Gazette*s themselves with the place and date of the deed are in WO 389. Armed with this information you can then find out more by using war diaries (see above).

The Distinguished Conduct Medal (DCM) was awarded to non-commissioned officers and other ranks. Gazette books are in WO 391, with a card index of holders in the Microfilm Reading Room at Kew. Recipients are also listed in R.W. Walker, *Recipients of the Distinguished Conduct Medal, 1914–1920* (Midland Records, 1981).

WAAC

The Army established the Women's Army Auxiliary Corps (WAAC) in March 1917 to undertake clerical and light manual work, thus releasing men for the front. In appreciation of its good services it was renamed the Queen Mary's Auxiliary Army Corps in April 1918. At its height in November 1918 the strength of the WAAC was more than 40,000. Altogether nearly 57,000 women served in the Corps but only about 9,000 records survive. These records have been arranged in surname order and so are relatively easy to use. They are available on microfilm in class WO 398. Their contents are not dissimilar to the service records for men. Officer equivalents were called 'officials', non-commissioned officers 'forewomen', and the rank and file 'workers'. An incomplete nominal roll for members of the Corps is in WO 162/16 with a list of women drivers employed during the war in WO 162/62. Recommendations for honours and awards are in WO 162/65.

OTHER SOURCES

COURTS MARTIAL

Nearly 300,000 soldiers and 6,000 officers faced courts martial during the war, generally for being absent without leave or drunkenness. Service records should indicate whether your ancestor was put on a charge. Registers of courts martial in WO 90 (for men serving overseas) and WO 92 (for men on home duty), will give brief details of the offence. Details of more serious offences can be found in registers in WO 213 and files in WO 71 and WO 93. More information is given in the National Archives leaflet *British Army: Courts Martial: First World War, 1914–1918* (Military Records Information 75).

Much has been made in recent years of the 306 men 'shot at dawn', often for (to modern eyes) trifling offences. Their story is told in Julian Putkowski and Julian Sykes, *Shot at Dawn* (Pen and Sword, 1998); the book also provides references to the court martial documents at the National Archives. A website devoted to the campaign to secure a pardon for these men is at www.shotatdawn.org.uk.

ELECTORAL REGISTERS

The Act of Parliament which gave women the vote in 1918 also extended the franchise to all servicemen, no matter how young they were. If they decided to register, men will appear in the Absent Voter part of the electoral registers. The registers will give you the address, the man's rank, unit and service number. If they survive, these records should be at the local record office or local studies library. For more information see Norman Holding, *More Sources of World War I Army Ancestry.*

MILITARY SERVICE TRIBUNALS

With the introduction of conscription an appeals system was established, which allowed men (and their employers) to appeal against being called up. The vast majority of cases concerned employment (such as the last young man on a farm) or domestic arrangements (looking after elderly relations). Only a few related to conscientious objections against the war and warfare in general. Most records of these tribunals were destroyed in the 1920s, with only the ones for Middlesex being preserved at the National Archives (in series MH 47) and for Midlothian at the National Archives of Scotland, HM General Register House, Edinburgh EH1 3YY (www.nas.gov.uk). Records from a few tribunals also survive at local record offices, so it is always worth asking. The loss of these records is more than made up for by full coverage in local newspapers, often including verbatim accounts of meetings and the decisions made by the tribunal. Sources for conscientious objectors are described in Chapter 6.

NATIONAL ROLL OF HONOUR

A unique and sadly incomplete record is the *National Roll of Honour*, which was published in the years after the war. It comprised short biographical descriptions of individuals, both men and women, civilians as well as servicemen. In most cases this is the only record of their war service. Volumes were issued for London, Southampton, Bradford, Luton, Birmingham, Leeds, Portsmouth, Manchester, Bedford and Northampton, and Salford. The Society of Genealogists (address in Appendix I) has a set. It has also been recently reprinted by the Naval and Military Press together with an index, so larger reference libraries may also have sets.

IRELAND

Only in recent years has Ireland's contribution to the British war effort been remembered, most notably with the dedication of the Irish War Memorial at Messines in November 1998 in the presence of the President of the Irish Republic and the Queen. Nearly 150,000 Irishmen served, even though conscription was never introduced for political reasons.

Records of deaths of men who came from the South are with the General Register Office, Joyce House, 8–11 Lombard St East, Dublin 2 (www.groireland.ie), while those for the North are with the General Register Office of Northern Ireland, Oxford House, 49–55 Chichester St, Belfast BT1 4HL (http://nisra.nics.gov.uk).

Records for Irish servicemen and the units they served with can be found in the same way as those from other parts of the British Isles. Records of the regiments which were disbanded on the formation of the Irish Free State in 1922, however, are with the National Army Museum in London (address in Appendix I).

Some 49,000 Irishmen who lost their lives are commemorated in *Ireland's Memorial Records* (8 vols, 1922, reprinted by Naval and Military Press, 2003). Entries are similar in format to *Soldiers Died* (in which the men also appear), but additional information is often given. In Northern Ireland, the Somme Heritage Centre commemorates the men from all over Ireland who fought at the battle, particularly the men of the 16th Division, which suffered huge casualties. The Centre also has a computerised database about those who fell during the battle. Somme Heritage Centre, Whitespots Country Park, 233 Bangor Road, Newtownards, County Down BT23 7PH (www.irishsoldier.org).

SCOTLAND

As Scottish highland and lowland regiments, and the men who served in them, were part of the British Army their records are exactly the same as their English equivalents. There are, however, a few purely Scottish sources, which may be of interest. Deaths of Scottish soldiers, together with their marriages and baptisms of their children, are with the General Register of Scotland, New Register House, Edinburgh EH1 3YT (www.gro-scotland.gov.uk). By the end of 2003 these records should be available on-line at www.scotlandspeople.gov.uk.

The National War Museum of Scotland has a number of collections relating to Scotland's military involvement in the First World War. They are in Edinburgh Castle, Edinburgh EH1 2NG; tel: 0131 225 7534; (www.nms.ac.uk/war/index.htm).

Scotland's war dead are honoured at the Scots National War Memorial, again situated in the precincts of Edinburgh Castle. More information can be found on its website www.snwm.org.

4

NAVAL AND MARINE

❧

ROYAL NAVY

In 1914 Britain had the largest and most powerful navy in the world. Yet it is a paradox that at the only major naval battle (at Jutland in May 1916) it failed to prove its dominance in an indecisive encounter with the German Grand Fleet. For many men the greatest enemy was boredom.

Although the Navy seemed well prepared at the outbreak of war, there were in fact a number of deep-seated problems, including resistance to new technological developments such as mines and the submarine, which Admiral Lord Beresford complained were 'underhand, unfair and damned un-English'. A number of innovations and improvements to the lives of the ratings (other ranks) had been made by the First Sea Lord, Admiral Sir John 'Jackie' Fisher. Unfortunately he resigned in 1915 over the transfer of ships from the Home Fleet to help the ill-fated Dardanelles Expedition.

As in the Army there was a clear divide between officers and ratings. An officer often entered the service at the age of 13 and studied initially at Osborne Naval College on the Isle of Wight before transferring to Dartmouth. He went to sea as a midshipman at 18, but during the war this might be reduced to 15. Few ratings and warrant officers were accepted as officers. Ratings traditionally joined as Seaman Boys, also at the age of 15, and received training on training ships such as HMS *Indefatigable* based in the Mersey, or at shore establishments like HMS *Ganges* at Shotley in Suffolk.

Conditions aboard were spartan, but were certainly better than they had been during the nineteenth century. By 1914, cutlery had been provided on the mess decks, and improved ventilation, bathrooms and

The destroyer HMS Princess Royal took part in the Battle of the Dogger Bank in early 1915 which stopped German ships shelling East Coast towns.

heating were provided below decks. Bakeries, for daily supplies of fresh bread, were installed on larger warships, as were libraries. Funds were raised during the war to provide travelling cinemas to give shows on-board ships.

The Navy's fighting qualities were not exemplified in fleet actions (of which there were very few), as much as in single-ship operations where skill and daring were given free rein. The exploits of British submariners were legendary. Max Horton, commanding submarine E9, terrorised German shipping in the Baltic to such an extent that the area became known as 'Horton's Sea' and the Germans resorted to recruiting a female assassin, who unfortunately for them succumbed to his charms.

Q-ships, which posed as unarmed merchantmen, were another way in which men could show their abilities under fire. 'Panic parties', for example, at first sight appeared to be seamen fleeing a sinking ship only to return fire when they got close to an attacking German U-boat.

For the most part during the latter stages of the war naval ships were engaged in the dull but vital task of protecting convoys bringing vital food and supplies from North America and further afield. Convoys were only introduced in 1917 after considerable opposition from the Admiralty. The new system dramatically cut the loss of merchant shipping from enemy attack.

The British North Sea Fleet at sea. Although the Royal Navy was the most powerful navy in the world, it found it difficult to defeat the German Navy, either in a conventional battle such as the one at Jutland in May 1916, or by sinking the U-boats which preyed on merchant shipping.

In the early months of the war the Navy had a surplus of 30,000 men. In response, the First Sea Lord, Winston Churchill, organised several brigades of the Naval Division, who fought alongside the Army initially defending Antwerp then later at Gallipoli and in Flanders. In 1916 the Division was transferred to the Army as 63rd (Royal Naval) Division. Despite the fact that the Division were operating in conditions very different from the high seas, naval discipline was maintained. Time continued to be regulated by bells as if aboard ship. Men referred to leaving the front line as 'going ashore'. There was also a long-running battle over the wearing of beards, which were prohibited in the Army, but allowed in the Navy. Indeed, the brigades themselves were named after naval heroes: Anson, Benbow (disbanded in 1916), Collingwood (disbanded in 1916), Drake, Hawke, Hood, Howe and Nelson.

An article about sailors who served in the Royal Navy during the First World War appeared in issue 71 of *Family History Monthly*. The records themselves are at the National Archives unless indicated.

SERVICE RECORDS

Records for officers who enlisted after 1917 are with Naval Correspondence, MoD Repository, Government Buildings, Bourne Ave, Hayes UB3 1RS. To be able to get access to them you will have to prove that you are the next of kin or descendant. The Ministry of Defence charges a fee for this service. In practice, however, most service records for officers and the non-commissioned warrant officers who served during the war are at the National Archives in ADM 196. You should find details of the officer's family and his date of birth, promotions and ships served on, together with brief notes about a man's performance. Another useful series are the summaries of confidential reports also in ADM 196, which contain candid comments on officers' abilities written by senior officers.

It is also worth looking at the officers' service cards in ADM 340. They were introduced early in the twentieth century for all officers then serving, including therefore some with service dating back to the 1880s. The information often duplicates that found elsewhere (particularly in the records in ADM 240), although they include officers who joined during the war and continued serving in some cases to the 1950s.

Records of ratings are in ADM 188. These records will tell you which ships a man served with, promotions and remarks about conduct. They are, however, arranged by branch in which an individual served, so it is a good idea to know what trade your ancestor was engaged in. Service records for ratings who were with a section of armoured cars in Russia between 1915 and 1917 are in ADM 116/529. The Fleet Air Arm Museum (address in Appendix I) has engagement books for men who joined between 1905 and 1921. These books include details of date and place of joining, physical description, details of any previous military service, and parent's consent if the entrant was a minor.

The Royal Navy had several reserve forces from which men were called up in time of war. The most important of these was the Royal Naval Reserve (RNR), whose men came from merchant ships. Officers' service records are in ADM 240 and they are also mentioned in the *Navy List*. Records of ratings are in BT 377/7, which is on microfiche in the Microfilm Reading Room. There are various series of indexes in BT 377. More about the RNR can be found in Chris and Michael Watts' *My Ancestor was a Merchant Seaman*. Many records for ratings can be found at the Fleet Air Arm Museum.

There was also the Royal Naval Volunteer Reserve (RNVR), whose members came from a much wider range of civilian occupations. Service records for RNVR officers are in ADM 337/117-128, with a card index available in the Microfilm Reading Room. Records for ratings are in ADM 337/1-108, arranged in service number order. If you do not already have the number you can quickly finding it by looking at the campaign medal rolls in ADM 171. Some records for ratings are also found at the Fleet Air Arm Museum.

Service records for officers in the Royal Naval Division (RND) are in ADM 339/3, with the equivalent for ratings in ADM 339/1, although records of ratings who died on active service are in ADM 339/2. War diaries for the brigades into which the Division was divided are in WO 95 and ADM 137.

All Royal Naval service records can be difficult to use, particularly when trying to identify which ledger is likely to contain details of your man. Guidance is given in Bruno Pappalardo, *Tracing Your Naval Ancestors* (PRO, 2003) and in the various free leaflets published by the National Archives and which can be downloaded from their website.

ROYAL MARINES

Royal Marine officers' records (including warrant officers) are in ADM 196, which give full details of service and include, in some cases, the name and profession of the officer's father. Officers are also listed in the Army and Navy Lists.

It is more difficult to trace the careers of ordinary marines. These records are arranged by the division in which they served, that is Chatham, Plymouth and Portsmouth. In addition, the Royal Marines were further divided between the Royal Marine Light Infantry (sometimes called the Red Marines) and the Royal Marine Artillery (Blue Marines). Service records are in ADM 159, which provide a marine's date and place of birth, trade, physical description, religion, date and place of enlistment and a full record of service with comments on conduct. They are arranged by division and then by service number. An index to service numbers is in ADM 313. In addition, there are attestation papers in ADM 157, which are loose forms, compiled for each marine on enlistment. They give birthplace, previous occupation, physical description and often a record of service. Description books in ADM 158 consist of several different types of register giving the date and place of enlistment, age, parish of birth, previous occupation, physical description, promotions and whether injured or killed.

In addition, some material about marines and their services is held at the Royal Marines Museum, Southsea PO4 9PX, (www. royalmarinesmuseum.co.uk). More about these records can be found in Garth Thomas, *Records of Royal Marines* (PRO Publications, 1994).

Many service records for men who served in the Chatham, Deal and Plymouth Divisions (but not Portsmouth) before and during the war are at the Fleet Air Arm Museum.

CASUALTIES

Royal Navy and Royal Marine officers and ratings who died during the First World War are listed in the War Graves Roll, in ADM 242. This gives full name, rank, service number, ship's name, date and place of birth, cause of death, where buried, and next of kin. There is a card index to these records in the Research Enquiries Room at Kew. Entries will give the name, date, place and cause of death of the deceased, which naval memorial his name is engraved on, and on occasion the person who has been informed of the death, which is usually the next of kin. Further registers of killed and wounded are in ADM 104/145-149.

In addition, naval casualties are listed in: S.D. and D.B. Jarvis, *The Cross of Sacrifice: Officers Who Died in the Service of the RN, RNVR, RM, RNAS and RAF, 1914–1919* (Naval and Military Press, 2000) and S.D. and D.B. Jarvis, *The Cross of Sacrifice: Non-Commissioned Officers, Men and Women of the UK, Commonwealth and Empire Who Died in the Service of the Royal Naval Air Service, Royal Navy, Royal Marines, Royal Flying Corps and Royal Air Force 1914–1921* (Naval and Military Press, 1996). The National Archives' and Society of Genealogists' libraries have copies of these books.

PRISONERS OF WAR

The difficulty of finding out about individual POWs has been mentioned in Chapter 3. The published *List of Officers taken Prisoner in the Various Theatres of War between August 1914 and November 1918* (1919, reprinted London Stamp Exchange, 1988) includes a number of naval officers. There is also some correspondence in ADM 1, ADM 116 and ADM 137, with an index in ADM 12 (code 79).

An illustration of a naval gun crew from The Queen's Gift Book, *sold in aid of soldiers and sailors who lost their limbs during the war. The ghost of Nelson was often evoked by propagandists of the time.*

OPERATIONAL RECORDS

It can be frustratingly difficult to track down reports and descriptions of activities during the First World War. Ships' log books (in ADM 53) normally only include weather and navigational details. Otherwise material might be found in three other series, although the electronic catalogue on the NA's website might be able to assist you in your search. It is best to start with series ADM 137, which contains most of the Admiralty papers for the period. If this is unsuccessful, try ADM 116 and then ADM 1. The volumes of indexes and digest in ADM 12, provide an index to all three series. However, it is so cumbersome to use that you will probably be best advised just to browse the class lists, especially as ADM 1 and ADM 116 are divided by subject. If you are interested, Bruno Pappalardo's *Tracing Your Naval Ancestors* explains how to use ADM 12.

MEDALS AND AWARDS

Naval personnel were entitled to the same campaign medals as their military counterparts. Rolls for these medals are in ADM 171 at the National Archives. Biographies of Naval VC winners and the reasons behind the award of the medal can be found in Stephen Snelling, *The Naval VCs of the First World War* (Sutton Publishing, 2002). ADM 171 also contains details of other medals awarded for gallantry.

WRNS

The Royal Navy in 1916 was the first service to recruit women to take over the role of cooks, clerks, wireless telegraphists, code experts and electricians, although it took until November 1917 to set up the Women's Royal Naval Service (WRNS). However, only 6,000 women served as Wrens. Two series of records exist. Service registers for the 438 officers in the service are in ADM 321 and a selection of personal files in ADM 318. Records for ratings (that is, other ranks) are in ADM 336. They are arranged in service number order, with an alphabetical index to names.

MERCHANT MARINE

In 1914 Britain had the largest merchant fleet in the world. British owned and crewed ships could be found in every port around the world.

The war took a heavy toll, with thousands of tons of shipping lost largely to German submarines, and 14,287 seamen lost their lives. Crew members came from all over the world, with significant numbers of Indians and West and East Africans. Indeed, only 60% of the men who died were British born. Virtually all officers, including the author's paternal grandfather, were British.

SERVICE RECORDS

Service records for men who served in the Merchant Navy during the First World War are virtually non-existent. Record cards from the Central Index Register, covering the period 1913 to 1920, were destroyed some time ago. All that survives are the cards from a special index for 1918 to 1921. Each card usually gives name, place and date of birth, a short description and a photograph of the man. If the seaman served beyond 1942, then the Central Register of Seamen, 1942–1972 may be of use. *Lloyd's Captains' Registers* can be used for information on masters and mates. There are also Certificates of Competency and Service (to 1921) at the National Archives. Successful applications for these certificates (to 1928) are held by the National Maritime Museum.

Agreements and crew lists show which men served on individual ships: a separate document was completed for each voyage. The NA has a 10% sample in BT 99, with an index to the ships at the enquiry desk in the Research Enquiries Room. Those for 1915 are with the National Maritime Museum. Lists for ships registered in Belfast are with the Public Record Office of Northern Ireland and those at Dublin in the National Archives of Ireland. The remainder (80% of the total) are with the Maritime History Archive, Memorial University of Newfoundland, St. John's, NL, A1C 5S7, Canada (www.mun.ca/mha). They will photocopy the appropriate documents for you for a small charge.

Logbooks contain details of a man's conduct on board and whether he became sick or died during the voyage. A very large collection can be found in BT 165.

CASUALTIES

There are a number of different sources which can used. It is probably best to start by checking the entry in S.B. and D.B. Jarvis, *The Cross of Sacrifice: Officers, Men and Women of the Merchant Navy and Mercantile Fleet Auxiliary, 1914–1919* (Naval and Military Press,

2000) before turning to record sources. The National Maritime Museum has returns of deaths, 1914–19; and at the NA there are the Registers of Deceased Seamen, 1914–18 (BT 334/62, 65, 67, 71 and 73) and a roll of honour in BT 339.

The Merchant Navy Association, PO Box 35, Torpoint, Cornwall PL11 2WD (www.mna.org.uk) may also be able to help. Their archive has complete records of all merchant seamen who lost their lives during wartime (full name, rating, ship, date and, often, age and home town), records of their ships, how their ships were lost (cause of loss, U-boat details, time and place of attack, voyage and cargo, references to official records at the National Archives and much more). A charge is made for checking these records.

PRISONERS OF WAR

A number of lists of merchant seamen and fishermen held prisoner by the Germans are in FO 383. A list of references is given in Chris and Michael Watts, *My Ancestor was a Merchant Seaman*. There is also a list of men taken prisoner in 1916 and 1917 in MT 9/1098.

OPERATIONAL RECORDS

It can be difficult to find very much about individual ships during the war, although you can normally pick up something about ships which were sunk. Such a list can be found in MT 25, with some courts of inquiry in BT 369 although many records have been lost. Some papers may be found in ADM 137. Outside the NA, Lloyd's Marine Collection, at the Guildhall Library in London, may well have material (address in Appendix I).

MEDALS AND AWARDS

Men of the Mercantile Marine Reserve, and officers and men of the Royal Naval Reserve, received the 1914-15 Star (if they had seen service before the end of 1915), the British War Medal and the Victory Medal. The Mercantile Marine War Medal was also awarded to those with sea service of not less than six months between 4th August 1914 and 11th November 1918, and who served at sea on at least one voyage through a danger zone. All those who received the MMWM were automatically entitled to receive the British War Medal; lists of recipients are at the National Archives in BT 351. Many seamen were awarded the Silver War Badge, which was given to all civilians engaged in war work. Lists of recipients are in MT 9 (code 6).

Merchant seamen were entitled to medals for gallantry, generally awarded for saving lives. The highest award was the Albert Medal for which there should be an announcement in the *London Gazette* – annotated copies can be found in BT 339/5, with other records in MT 9 (code 6). There are also some records in MT 9. Registers of men awarded the Sea Gallantry Medal are in BT 261. Again there should be an announcement in the *London Gazette*, with additional records in MT 9 (code 6). The National Archives has copies (in series ZJ 1) together with indexes in the Microfilm Reading Room. Copies of the *Gazette* may also be found in other libraries and digitised copies are available on-line at www.gazettes-online.co.uk.

OTHER SOURCES

Shipping companies often kept records of their employees. However, many companies amalgamated or were taken over by rivals particularly after the Second World War; consult the National Register of Archives at the National Archives (see Appendix I for address). Some records are described in Peter Mathias and A.W.H. Pearsall, *Shipping: A Survey of Historical Records* (David and Charles, 1971), although the book is now very dated.

FURTHER READING

There are few studies about the Merchant Marine during the First World War, which is somewhat surprising considering the vital role it played in supplying Britain with food, munitions and servicemen from the dominions. There is an interesting essay by Tony Lane on the merchant seaman's experience of the war in Hugh Cecil's and Peter Liddle's *Facing Armageddon*. John Terraine's *Business in Great Waters: the U-Boat Wars* (Leo Cooper, 1989) describes the developing U-boat campaigns against British shipping. There are also three volumes of an official history on *The Merchant Navy* and a further four volumes devoted to *The Seaborne Trade*. Fortunately, there are several excellent research guides to service records (for details see Appendix IV).

Sage advice about tracing merchant seamen ancestors can be found at www.barnettresearch.freeserve.co.uk/main.htm.

5

THE AIR SERVICES

꙳

The Balloon Section of the Royal Engineers was established as long ago as 1879, to provide reconnaissance balloons for use in colonial campaigns and later in the Boer War. Flying in Britain, however, was slow to develop. The American showman 'Colonel' Samuel F. Cody made the first flight in this country on 16th October 1908 at Farnborough. The military planners were less than impressed with this new technology. In a report for the Committee of Imperial Defence in 1909, Lord Esher recommended that the Navy be allowed £35,000 to build an experimental airship and the Army £10,000 for experiments on navigable balloons. Esher, however, saw 'no necessity for the Government to continue experiments in aeroplanes provided that advantage is taken of private enterprise in this form of aviation'.

One example of this was the training undertaken by the Royal Aero Club on behalf of the Army. Successful students had their fees refunded on their joining the Royal Flying Corps (RFC). The Corps itself was formed in 1912, combining existing army and navy flying activities. In July 1914, the naval wing broke away to become the Royal Naval Air Service (RNAS): wags claimed that the abbreviation stood for Really Not A Sailor. On the outbreak of war a month later the four squadrons of the RFC, totalling 105 officers, 63 aeroplanes and 95 lorries, were sent to France. Left at home were 116 aircraft (described as 'mainly junk'), 41 officers and a few hundred airmen.

The First World War saw a rapid expansion in the air services and the work undertaken by aircraft. The RFC spent much of its time offering support to the Army on the Western Front and elsewhere by initially operating reconnaissance missions, and later through artillery spotting, and bombing German targets in Belgium. The RNAS was responsible for the air defence of Britain until February 1916 (when it was transferred to the RFC), and was the pioneer of strategic bombing against Germany and sites in occupied Belgium from its base in Dunkirk. In addition, the Service operated patrols from coastal air stations in Britain and from ships, including by 1918 the first aircraft carriers.

The mobility and freedom of the air was often contrasted with the stalemate of the trenches, particularly by the media. Even so the lives of pilots and observers were usually merry and often short. In 1917 the life expectancy of a pilot on the Western Front was between eleven days and three weeks.

One man who survived these long odds – only to die in the Spanish Flu pandemic a week after the Armistice – was Lt Col Leoline Jenkins (1891-1918). Before the war Jenkins was a schoolmaster at his old prep school at Durlston Court, Swanage in Dorset. He joined the RFC in 1915 and was posted to 15 Squadron in France just before Christmas that year. During 1916 and 1917 he flew many missions, winning the Distinguished Service Order (DSO) and the Military Cross (MC) and bar (that is, a second award of the medal). A friend wrote of him:

> He used to fly alone (from preference), put as much armoured protection as he could on his plane and then after flying high, swoop down like a hawk close to the German guns... I suppose that after the experiences of being potted at by small boys' questions in the close range of a Durlston classroom, the bullets of the Huns are of minor consequences. There is not much of the "Wait and see" about L.J.

These heroics charmed the British people, who for much of the war had little else to cheer about. Unfortunately neither the RFC nor the RNAS were particularly successful when it came to stopping German Zeppelin airship raids on British cities. Aircraft found it very difficult to locate and shoot down these huge airships. The damage caused by the raids was mainly psychological rather than actual, yet it was enough for considerable pressure to be brought upon the politicians to do something. Committees were established which found that a major problem was the lack of co-ordination between the RFC and RNAS, coupled with a waste of valuable resources.

Despite considerable opposition from the Army and the Navy the new Royal Air Force was formed on 1st April 1918, merging the two air services. RNAS squadrons had the prefix 2 or 20 added to their number: 4 RNAS Squadron for example became 204 Squadron.

The RFC was rather larger than its naval cousin so inevitably played the dominant role. In June an Independent Force was established with the sole purpose of bombing strategic targets in Germany and a number of fairly ineffectual raids carried out. By November 1918 the Royal Air Force had 188 squadrons, with 22,467 aircraft and 103 airships on strength, and 27,000 officers and 264,000 other ranks including 25,000 women.

SOURCES

The majority of aviation records for the First World War are with the National Archives, and are largely found in one series, AIR 1. Even with electronic catalogues the series is not the easiest to use. In particular (and most unusually) you need to use the former Air Historical Branch (AHB) reference as well as the NA piece number when you order a document. So if, for example, you want to look at a list of airmen who won the Victoria Cross you need to have both the NA reference (AIR 1/519) and the AHB number (16/9/1).

In particular, the NA has personnel records for men who served in the various air services roughly up to the end of 1920. As might be expected there is considerably more about pilots, navigators, and observers than about the engineering staff who maintained the aircraft or the clerical staff working behind the scenes.

David J. Barnes is compiling an on-line roll of the men who served in the RFC, RNAS and RAF, together with as much biographical detail as possible. More about this project can be found at www.rfc-rnas-raf-register.org.uk, or write to him at 148 Parkinson Street, Burnley BB11 3LL.

In your research it is also worth checking the sources described in Chapter 3 for the Army (for the RFC) and Chapter 4 for the Navy (RNAS). Chapter 3 also includes material of interest to researchers in general.

SERVICE RECORDS: PRE-APRIL 1918

Men who joined the RFC between its formation in 1912 and August 1914 (service numbers 1–1400) are described in J. V. Webb and I. McInnes, *The Contemptible Little Flying Corps*. The NA has a copy of the book. If their service ended before 1 April 1918 there will be nothing in the RAF records: you will need to use WO 338 and WO 364 (for the RFC) and ADM 188/560-646 (for RNAS ratings). Records of RNAS officers can be found in ADM 273, arranged in service number order There is a card index to these records in the Research Enquiries Room at Kew. As an Admiralty conceit, men in the RNAS may be referred to as being on the strength of the shore based HMS *Pembroke*.

RAF SERVICE RECORDS

The NA has service records for RAF officers and airmen who were discharged before the early 1920s. It's not possible to be specific as there is no clear cut off date. Later records are held by the Ministry of Defence, PMA (CS) 2a2, Building 248a, HQ RAF PYC, RAF Innsworth GL3 1EZ. To be able to get access to them you will have to prove that you are the next of kin or descendant. The Ministry of Defence charges a fee for this service, currently (2003) £25.

Service records for RAF officers until the early 1920s are in series AIR 76 arranged in surname order. They include details about next of kin, civilian occupation, units in which an individual served, appointments and promotions, and honours and medals awarded. In addition, comments may have been added by training officers about the individuals' flying skills or (more likely) lack of them. These records are available in the Microfilm Reading Room. Curiously, alternate pages have been filmed upside down which can cause problems navigating through a film! On the formation of the RAF a new *Air Force List* was published on the lines of the Army and Navy Lists, which included brief details of officers. The only copy that the NA has for the period of the First World War is for April 1918.

The war service of many pilots, particularly those regarded as 'aces' (that is who shot down five or more enemy aircraft) have been researched and published in books, such as C. F. Shores, N. L. R. Franks and R. Guest, *Above the Trenches. A Complete Record of the Fighter Aces and Units of the British Empire Air Forces, 1915–1920*. A list of such books can be found in Appendix IV.

Early pilots were trained by civilian air schools and received the Royal Aero Club's Aviator's Certificate. The RAF Museum (for address see Appendix I) has a card index to the holders of these certificates, with date of birth, address, profession and where and when he qualified. Pilots were also obliged to submit a portrait photograph with their application and these also largely survive.

Records of other RAF ranks are in AIR 79. They are arranged in service number order with indexes in AIR 78. Apart from personal details, these records include dates of enlistment and discharge, promotions and postings, medical and disciplinary history, and details of medals awarded. These records are on microfilm, which can be seen in the Microfilm Reading Room.

In addition, the NA has two copies of a muster roll of all other ranks that was compiled in early April 1918, in AIR 1/819 and AIR 10/232-237. The roll is arranged in service number order.

CASUALTIES

The Imperial War Museum (for details see Appendix I) has a roll of honour for members of the RFC and RNAS who died during the war. Both the RAF Museum and the Imperial War Museum have copies of Capt G.C. Campbell's *Royal Flying Corps: Casualties and Honours during the War 1914–1917* which lists pilots and navigators (officers only) who died between 1914 and 1917. This can be a useful source as airmen and officers do not appear in *Soldiers Died in the Great War*. The *London Gazette* provides more information of other ranks who died on active service. Brief details of the service of non-commissioned officers and men appears in S.B. and D.B. Jarvis, *The Cross of Sacrifice: Non-Commissioned Officers, Men and Women of the UK, Commonwealth and Empire Who Died in the Service of the Royal Naval Air Service, Royal Navy, Royal Marines, Royal Flying Corps and Royal Air Force 1914–1921* (Naval and Military Press, 1996) and Chris Hobson, *Airmen Died in the Great War 1914–1918; The Roll of Honour of the British and Commonwealth Air Services of the First World War* (4 vols, Savannah Publications, 1998).

Reports of aircraft (and pilot) casualties on the Western Front between March 1916 and April 1919 are in AIR 1/843-860, 865, and other lists in AIR 1/914-916, 960-969. The RAF Museum holds an extensive set of record cards relating to deaths, injuries and illness suffered by Royal Flying Corps and Royal Air Force personnel (and ex-Royal Naval Air Service after 1 April 1918). They cover the period roughly between 1915 and 1928. They were originally arranged in different series for a variety of purposes, now unclear. These cards cover circumstances from off-duty sporting accidents to deaths.

The records are not complete but a variable amount of information can be gleaned from them. Some cards record the movements of prisoners of war or give Court of Enquiry summaries for accidents occurring in the United Kingdom. Details recorded for other ranks are usually much briefer than those for officers. Serial numbers and types of aircraft are sometimes given.

The Museum also holds Medical Board record cards covering the dates 1917–1920 approximately. These cards record attendance at medical boards and diagnosis for officers of the RFC and Royal Air Force.

Information about the officers and ratings of the RNAS who died during the war are in ADM 242. There is an index (officers only) in the Research Enquiries Room. In addition S.B. and D.B. Jarvis, *The Cross of Sacrifice: Officers who Died in the Service of the Royal Navy . . . RNAS and RAF, 1914–1919* (Naval and Military Press, 2000) describes the careers of RNAS and RAF officers who died on active service during the war. The Fleet Air Arm Museum is preparing a roll of honour for RNAS personnel which eventually will be placed in a local church.

OPERATIONAL RECORDS

The RAF Museum at Hendon (for address see Appendix I) also has a nearly complete set of RFC and (later) RAF official communiqués; that is, weekly summaries of activities, which were published by headquarters. They describe individual missions, including the shooting down of enemy aircraft and bombing raids and the names of pilots and squadrons involved. The National Archives also has an incomplete set in AIR 1. They have also been republished (see Appendix IV for details).

Almost all surviving records for both the RFC and RNAS are in series AIR 1, often arranged by squadron. For most squadrons, and some other units, there are operational record books which give some idea of what happened day by day. Reports and other operational records for the RNAS are in ADM 137. Diaries (known as line books) describing the activities of many RNAS units are with the Fleet Air Arm Museum (see Appendix I for address).

There may also be other records that can shed light on a man's career as a pilot or navigator, such as lists of property forwarded to next of kin or combat reports compiled after a German aircraft had been shot down. Combat reports are particularly valuable, although they should be treated with some caution, as pilots tended to claim planes which they had seen shot down. The British claimed over 7,000 victories from June 1916 to the Armistice, yet German records show they only lost 3,000 aircraft. Few logbooks are at the NA (look in AIR 4 for aircraft and AIR 3 for airships), but the RAF Museum has a reasonable collection.

Many squadrons and other units produced magazines which also give an idea of life in the unit. The largest collection of these is held by the RAF Museum.

MEDALS AND AWARDS: GALLANTRY

It can be difficult to find information about gallantry awards made to RFC, RNAS and RAF personnel. They are gazetted in the *London Gazette*, but after the middle of 1916 rarely contain citations. There are files containing citations which were presented to the King for his approval in making the award in class AIR 2 (code 30), with others in WO 373. There is no index, although Paul Baillie, 14 Wheatfields, St Ives PE17 6YD has been compiling one for many years.

MEDALS AND AWARDS: CAMPAIGN

Record cards for men in both the RFC and RAF who were awarded the British War and Victory Medals are on microfiche in the Microfilm Reading Room at Kew. For more details see chapter 3. The equivalent for the RNAS is in ADM 171/89-91, 94-119. In using these records it may help to know that RNAS personnel were technically on the strength of HMS *Pembroke* until 2nd February 1915 when they were transferred to HMS *President* and other shore bases.

The sources available for medals, both campaign and gallantry, are well described in William Spencer, *Air Force Records for Family Historians*.

WRAF

When the new Royal Air Force was established on 1st April 1918 it included a small component of women known as the Women's Royal Air Force (WRAF); by November 1918 some 25,500 were in the service. Only records for other ranks in the WRAF survive. They are to be found in AIR 80. They are arranged alphabetically by surname and so are easy to use.

6

WOMEN AND CIVILIANS

❧

Within weeks of the outbreak of the First World War a respected
Scottish doctor, Elsie Inglis, went to the War Office in London to offer
her services at the front where medical staff were already in short
supply. Her offer was declined by an official who patronisingly told her,
'Dear lady, go home and keep quiet'.

Spurned by the British, Dr Inglis established the Scottish Women's
Hospital committee which sent all-women hospital units to the front.
Undeterred by the primitive conditions, she organised a number of
hospitals to look after Serbian troops, who were fighting alongside
British troops against the Austrians. According to the Prefect of
Constanza, 'It is extraordinary how these women endure hardships; they
refuse help, and carry the wounded themselves. They work like navvies.
No wonder England is a great country if the women are like that'.

The almost forgotten heroism of Elsie Inglis is just one example of
the commitment shown by women to the war effort during the First
World War, from driving buses to serving in the forces, often
undertaking work that would have been unthinkable in peacetime. As a
result, by the Armistice the attitude towards women, and what they
could do, had changed totally. The moderate suffragette Millicent
Garrett Fawcett wrote in 1920 that 'the war revolutionised the position
of women. It found them serfs and left them free'. Their reward was the
vote which was granted to all women (over the age of 30) in February
1918.

Even so it should be remembered that relatively few women took up
war work. At a time when it was customary for women to stop work on
their marriage it was difficult for wives, let alone mothers, to find
suitable employment. Most women who undertook war work were
young and single. For most it was the chance of a lifetime to escape the

73

During 1917 and 1918 displays of tanks in town centres were familiar sights helping to boost war savings and other schemes. Somewhere in this picture of the crowd milling around this tank next to the Guildhall in Norwich is my great-aunt who is enlisting in the Women's Land Army.

confines of a normal life. And although conditions could be primitive many enjoyed their experience. An Army telegraphist, Dorothy Mary Bruce, recalled in 1992 that 'I have always looked back on it as my one adventure'.

WOMEN IN THE ARMED FORCES

Before the war women, apart from a few nurses, were excluded from service in either the Army or the Navy. The Royal Navy in 1916 was the first service to recruit women taking over the role of cooks, clerks, wireless telegraphists, code experts and electricians, although it took until November 1917 to set up the Women's Royal Naval Service (WRNS). The Army noted the success of the Navy's experiment and established the Women's Army Auxiliary Corps (WAAC) in March 1917 to undertake similar work, thus releasing men for the front. At its height in November 1918 the strength of the WAAC was over 40,000. Altogether nearly 57,000 women served in the Corps. The naval and air force women's services were rather smaller: 25,500 served with the WRAF and less than 6,000 with the WRNS.

The armed forces were not really equipped to deal with the women volunteers, as facilities were generally poor. But the welcome from the ordinary Tommy or Jack was warm. Indeed, the fear of the opposite sex led to the imposition of strict rules about conduct. In the WAAC alcohol was forbidden – except when prescribed for medicinal purposes – and no member was allowed to visit a bar. In addition women were chaperoned on their rare trips outside the bases in which they were serving. All these precautions did not stop the women's services developing a quite unfounded reputation for sexual licence. In 1918 the new commandant of the WAAC, Florence Burleigh Leach, had to swear an affidavit stating that to her knowledge no member of the Corps was being used for immoral purposes.

Despite the hard work, long hours and suspicion by the authorities, women in the services found a new freedom and most greatly enjoyed their time in uniform. One former WAAC wrote in 1927 that 'We had such a ripping time for more than two years, apart from the poor dears who were killed of course. . .'.

RECORDS OF SERVICEWOMEN

Surviving records for the three services are now largely at the National Archives, which are briefly described in a downloadable leaflet *Women's Services, First World War* (Military Records Information 74) and in the appropriate place elsewhere in this book.

Apart from the service records, perhaps the most useful record held by the NA is the microfiche of the rolls of the Women's Service Medal, which is to be found in the Microfilm Reading Room. It lists members of the WAAC and WRAF who were entitled to the various campaign medals, in particular the British War and Victory Medals which were issued to all servicewomen. The information given is not dissimilar to their male equivalents, with service number, theatres of operation served in and perhaps a note about when the medal was issued. Equivalent medal records for the WRNS may be found in ADM 171/93 also in the Microfilm Reading Room.

Apart from these records, finding out anything about these units and the people who served in them can be difficult. A number of former members have deposited personal papers either with the Imperial War Museum or the Liddle Collection in Leeds (addresses in Appendix I).

NURSING

By the middle of 1917 some 45,000 nurses were serving in the armed forces and thousands more women were doing auxiliary work in hospitals at home and in France. Before the war both the Army (Queen Alexandra's Imperial Military Nursing Service, QAIMNS) and the Navy (Queen Alexandra's Royal Army Nursing Corps, QARNC) had maintained small nursing services, which were greatly expanded after 1914. In addition the British Red Cross Society and the Order of St John had in 1909 set up a nationwide network of Voluntary Aid Detachments (VAD) comprising men and women who would help in hospitals and provide other assistance on the outbreak of war. These

Three nurses – the one on the right is my grandmother, Grace Elizabeth Crozier.

76

people became known as VADs. The sacrifice and heroism of both nurses and VADs soon entered the popular imagination. Vera Brittain, who worked as a VAD, remembered a trip across France with the troops waving and cheering as the nurses travelled by.

For all its popularity, nursing was frequently physically hard work and emotionally exhausting. Vera Brittain thought that, 'Adaptability, sympathy and magnetism of temperament count for more than the ability to bandage or make foods'.

RECORDS OF NURSES

Considerable records exist for nurses and VADS during the war. In addition there is a leaflet from the National Archives, which describe the records in detail. Nurses and VADs were entitled to the British War and Victory Medals and entries for them will be found in the Medal Index Cards at Kew. A number of nurses won the Royal Red Cross for especial devotion to duty. Registers for this medal are in WO 145 and recipients were noted in the Army and Navy Lists.

Patients in the ballroom at the Star and Garter Home, Richmond. This old hotel opened in 1916 as a home to care for incurably wounded servicemen. (Royal Star and Garter Home)

Service records for Army nurses, including members of the Territorial Forces Nursing Service, are in WO 399. Records of nurses who served with the QAIMNS may contain details of service, enrolment and discharge papers, and correspondence relating to the period of service. The list gives forename and surname. Pension records for nurses who served with QAIMNS are in PMG 34 while records for nurses who were awarded disability pensions are in PMG 42.

Service records for either RAF or Navy nurses have yet to be transferred to the National Archives. They are still with the Ministry of Defence, Bourne Ave, Hayes UB3 9RE, although I understand that they contain very little personal information. Some personal information about Navy nurses, however, can be found in ADM 104/96, 162-165.

Record cards for the many thousands of women who served as VADs during the war are with the Red Cross Archives, 9 Grosvenor Square, London SW1X 7EJ. Similar records for women who served with the Order of St John are with the Museum and Library, Order of St John, St John's Gate, St John's Lane, London EC1M 4DA.

CHARITY WORK

More women undertook voluntary work for one or more war charity or other organisation than any other war work. Some four million women knitted garments and bandages for the troops at the front, while hundreds of thousands of others helped collect eggs to go to hospitals for wounded soldiers and sailors. Many of the ladies who helped the war charities were too old or had family commitments that prevented them from participating more actively in the war effort. Women in the Dominions and British communities abroad also knitted for the troops or sent parcels of comforts to the home country.

RECORDS

It is nearly impossible to find much information about individual women. Wartime charitable activity was often covered in some detail by local newspapers. These reports and occasional photographs often list the people who helped at a bazaar or members of a knitting circle.

The one exception is for the few charity workers who served in France, generally running YMCA huts and refreshment buffets for soldiers. These were enormously popular facilities with the men who relished the atmosphere away from the war and the chance to spend a few minutes in female company, which reminded so many of home. The volunteers were entitled to the Victory and British War medals and their details can be found in the Medal Index Cards at the NA.

FACTORIES, FARMS AND TRANSPORT

As men departed for the front their places were increasingly taken by women. By August 1915 nearly a million women had entered the workforce. The first industry to specifically recruit women in any great numbers was the munitions factory. 'Munitionettes' as the lady workers were called were known for their high spending, for wages were high to compensate for the poor working conditions, and the peculiar yellow colour of their skins caused by the high explosives they were handling.

But for most people at the time the biggest surprise was the increasing number of women employed on the buses and on the railways. By the end of the war about a third of all railway staff were serving in the forces; their places were very largely taken by women as cleaners, porters, station staff and clerical workers. Women were eventually to be found everywhere, although few were doing anything more than menial or relatively unskilled work.

By the end of the war perhaps a quarter of a million girls had joined the Women's Land Army. The Army had been started in 1915, as the Women's Land Service Corps, but they found considerable hostility from both farmers and local villagers suspicious of incomers.

THE RECORDS

The survival of records for women employed in factories or on the land is very patchy. The best source is probably company magazines or trade journals which often include captioned photographs and lists of staff at one function or another. A typical example is the *Cocoa Works Times,* the works journal of Rowntrees in York which can be found at the Borthwick Institute, Peaseholme Green, York YO1 2PW. The National Archives has a set of railway magazines in the ZPER series that are full of interesting snippets about female workers. Also at the NA are the surviving railway company records, in the RAIL series, in which can be found staff registers and other material relating to employees.

Some records relating to munitions factories and the people who worked in them can be found at the NA in class MUN 5, but there is very little about individual workers.

By 1915 women were beginning to take over many of the jobs formerly undertaken by men.

Again, few records of the Women's Land Army survive and so far as I know no service records for the period are in existence. The NA has a few records in class MAF 42 and NATS 1, with some photographs in MAF 59.

Another unusual source is the *National Roll of Honour*, which recorded the war efforts of women as well as men. For more details see Chapter 3.

RECORDS FOR OTHER NON-COMBATANTS

CONSCIENTIOUS OBJECTORS

During the war there were 16,100 registered conscientious objectors. Some were given total exemption but the majority were placed in non-combatant corps, put to work in labour camps run by the Home Office, or to other works of national importance. Those who failed with their appeal to a Tribunal were sent to fight in France. Where they continued with their objection, they were imprisoned, court-martialled or worse: 1,298 conscientious objectors were imprisoned and 41 were executed. Records of the courts martial of these men are in WO 90 and 213. However, 1,350 'absolutists' refused this compromise and were imprisoned often in appalling conditions – 73 died while in prison. The cases of all these men were heard before military service tribunals (see Chapter 3), and extensively reported in local newspapers. There is no comprehensive list of conscientious objectors, although a National Archives leaflet *First World War: Conscientious Objectors & Exemptions from Service* (Military Records Information 16) describes the sources available at the NA. There is also material at the Imperial War Museum and the Society of Friends Library, Friends House, 173 Euston Road, London NW1 2BJ (www.quaker.org.uk/library/libenq.html). The Peace Pledge Union also has some records and they can be contacted at 41b Brecknock Road, London N7 0BT (wwww.plu.org.uk).

INTERNEES: BRITISH IN GERMANY

At the outbreak of war British and Commonwealth civilians resident in Germany were interned in camps, the largest of which was Ruhleben, a former racetrack on the edge of Berlin, which housed 4,500 men and women. Conditions were reasonable, considering the problems faced

MRS G.T. DAVIS

MRS W. LLOYD

MISS MAY BROOKS

MRS A.J. OXFORD

MRS GARDINER
SPECIAL
HONOURABLE
MENTION.

MRS W. GEE
ORGANISER OF
WHIST DRIVES

MRS E.L. WHITE

MRS W. HOBSON

MRS W. HAINE

OUR WORKERS

Some of the helpers of the Burton upon Trent Prisoners of War Fund.

82

by civilians in Germany as a whole: the biggest problem was boredom, which was overcome to an extent by a network of clubs and adult education classes.

It is now hard to find out very much about these people. A few lists can be found in the correspondence of the Foreign Office Prisoner of War Department (FO 383). There is a card index to these records in the Research Enquiries Room, so it is easy to check whether there is anything. The Imperial War Museum (address in Appendix I) also has some records in the Women's War Work Committee and elsewhere. Internees who died during the war are recorded on the Commonwealth War Graves Commission Debt of Honour roll (see Chapter 3 for more details).

The International Committee of the Red Cross (ICRC) in Geneva was responsible for passing details of civilians (both British and German) between the various combatant nations and ensuring that conditions in the camps were adequate. Voluminous records were maintained which are closed for 100 years, however their archivists will search the records for you. You need to contact the ICRC Archives, 19 avenue de la Paix, CH-1202 Genève, Switzerland. More information can be found at www.icrc.org.

INTERNEES: GERMANS IN BRITAIN

Similarly, the 60,000 German and Austrian citizens in Britain were also interned or repatriated. The largest internment camp was at Knockaloe near Peel on the Isle of Man, which housed 24,500 people. Lists of enemy aliens so interned are in HO 144 and WO 900, with related correspondence in HO 45. It is understood that personal files for these people have been destroyed: other records are held by the Red Cross in Geneva (see above). The Manx archives have no records either, although there is an interesting web page on Knockaloe at www.isle-of-man.com/manxnotebook/fulltext/sh1920/ch06.htm.

7

COMBATANTS FROM OTHER NATIONS

The war had profound effects on other nations, apart from Britain. It's all too easy to forget that German mothers' sons died in France, the fiancés of Italian girls laid down their lives in the Alps, and French and Serb husbands failed to return from Salonika. And, indeed, although British losses were horrendous they were nothing as compared to other nations: Germany, Russia and France proportionally all suffered worse casualties. The country that suffered the most was actually New Zealand, ironically the combatant furthest from Europe.

In this chapter we look at the major sources used to find out about the soldiers who fought in the other armies. In part this is done in a spirit of internationalism, but also because a large proportion of readers are likely to have had parents and grandparents who fought in armies other than the British. My maternal grandfather, Feldwebel (Corporal) Ismael Schoenwald, for example, was severely wounded while in the German Army and, according to my mother, was awarded an Iron Cross.

Christina K. Schaefer's *The Great War: A Guide to the World's Fighting Men* is undoubtedly the best source for further information, although she doesn't mention many of the resources that are now available on-line, which can largely be found by visiting www.cyndislist.com. Another important book is Philip J. Haythornthwaite's *The World War One Source Book.*

BRITISH EMPIRE

The colonies, which had largely been settled by British people (Australia, Canada, Newfoundland, South Africa and New Zealand), had received what was called dominion status that gave, in effect, independence, although foreign (and to a lesser extent, defence) policy was decided in Whitehall usually with only cursory consultation.

There was also the semi-autonomous Indian Empire (now India, Pakistan and Bangladesh), which was run by the British under a Viceroy. The Raj was made up of British-controlled India and a number of nominally independent native states, although here the dominant figure was always the British Resident. The British Army maintained a number of garrisons in the sub-continent. In addition there was the separate Indian Army, under the control of the Viceroy and largely officered by British officers.

Lastly there were dozens of different colonies, some of which had been British since the seventeenth century, while others in Africa and the Pacific had been annexed fairly recently. Most were poor and generally contributed little to the Empire, except perhaps occupying a strategic position or supplying raw materials such as rubber or tin for factories in Britain.

When Britain declared war on 4th August 1914 she did so on behalf of the Empire as well as the home islands. The declaration was generally warmly received. The Australian politician Andrew Fisher promised that, 'Australians will stand beside [the mother country] to help and defend her to our last man and our last shilling.' Indeed, the first shots of the war fired by a British unit were across the bows of an escaping German steamer during the afternoon of 5th August from a battery at the entrance of Port Philip Bay near Melbourne.

Troops from the Dominions distinguished themselves in every theatre of war: most notably at Gallipoli and in a series of battles on the Western Front, particularly Pozières on the Somme in 1916 (Australians) and Vimy Ridge in 1917 (Canadians). In the early days of the war Australian and New Zealand forces captured the German colonies in the Pacific, while South African troops fought a short campaign in German South West Africa (now Namibia). In addition there were small naval forces and air services.

The strains of war soon began to tell. In South Africa there was a short-lived rebellion by Boer nationalists. In Australia and Canada there were divisive debates about the need to introduce conscription in order to boost numbers of men being sent to Europe.

Behind the scenes there was increasing disquiet about the quality of British generalship, which saw thousands of troops needlessly sacrificed. In turn the British high command had reservations about the relaxed attitude to discipline and relations between officers and men which were common in the forces from the dominions. By 1918 however, Sir Arthur Currie from Canada and Sir John Monash from Australia were commanding exclusively Canadian and ANZAC corps on the Western Front respectively, reflecting both the contribution made by their nations as well as personal military qualities. Monash, who had been an estate agent before the war, was particularly highly regarded.

Dominion politicians were also increasingly drawn into the direction of the war. During 1917 and 1918 an Imperial War Council met in London, and General Jan Smuts (a former rebel Boer leader from South Africa) became a member of the War Cabinet. Meantime there was an insatiable demand for produce from the Empire, such as meat and horses from Australia and New Zealand, grain and munitions from Canada, and raw materials from the colonies.

A large proportion of the Dominion forces were made up of British-born men who had emigrated overseas before the war, but still felt a loyalty to the mother country. In addition a fair number of British men endeavoured to join these units, largely because pay and conditions were better than in the British Army as a whole. Conversely, Dominion-born men, who may have been working or studying in Britain, enlisted in British units. Nearly a thousand American volunteers also slipped across the 49th parallel to enlist in the Canadian forces, while others joined the RFC and RNAS.

Indian troops were rushed to France in 1914, where they served with distinction, until they were withdrawn in 1916 to serve in the disastrous Mesopotamian campaign. *The Times* commented in October 1914: 'The instinct which makes us such sticklers for propriety made us more reluctant than other nations to employ coloured troops against a white enemy' but as Japan was an ally and the French were using North African troops, the paper considered that it would not be fair to refuse the Indian Army 'the privilege of taking its place beside British troops'. This feeling of racism also permeated the employment of West Indian troops. Two battalions of the West India Regiment who served in France were largely employed in labour duties and obstacles were placed in the way of West Indians who wanted to enlist in British regiments.

With the exception of the Indian Army, contingents from the Dominions and colonies were regarded as being part of the British services. The records thus created are very similar to those you may be familiar with when researching British servicemen.

If your ancestor died in action while serving as an officer in a dominion or colonial regiment then you should be able to find out more

Indian troops baking Naan bread. In 1914 and 1915 Indian regiments fought with distinction in France and Flanders, before being transferred to Mesopotamia.

about his career in S.B. and D.B. Jarvis, *The Cross of Sacrifice: Officers Who Died in the Service of the Commonwealth and Colonial Regiments and Corps,, 1914–1919* (Naval and Military Press, 2000). The Commonwealth War Graves Commission also has details of all men from the dominions and colonies who lost their lives during the war. For more information see Chapter 3.

AUSTRALIA

The National Archives of Australia holds the records of the 1st AIF, Australian Flying Corps, Australian Naval and Military Expeditionary Force, Royal Australian Naval Bridging Train, Australian Army Nursing Service, and Depot, or home records, for personnel who served within Australia. For a fee a copy of the whole original record will be provided. If a soldier participated in both world wars, the record has often been combined in a Second World War file. Navy service records typically consist of one or two cardboard index cards with indistinct pencil notations. They are supplied free. Write to the First World War Personnel Records Service, National Archives of Australia, PO Box 7425, Canberra Mail Centre, ACT 2610.

The Australian equivalent to the Imperial War Museum is the Australian War Memorial (AWM), which has a superb collection of material relating to Australian forces since 1901. In particular there is an on-line roll of honour with some personnel details, based on forms supplied by next of kin to the AWM after the First World War, and a number of downloadable leaflets, possibly the most useful is *Australians who Served: First World War Records:* Australian War Memorial, GPO Box 345, Canberra, ACT 2601 (website: www.awm.gov.au).

The Australian Defence Force Academy manages a research and public education facility called the AIF Project. This is a computerised database listing the details of those who served overseas with the 1st Australian Imperial Force between 1914 and 1919. Access to the database is available to members of the public. For a fee they can provide a consolidated statement of service suitable for framing, plus a printout of the individual's information held on the database. For further information and order forms, contact: The AIF Project, School of History, University College, Australian Defence Force Academy, Canberra, ACT 2600.

An informative article about the Australians (and New Zealanders) during the war appeared in the February 2002 issue of *Family History Monthly* (No 77).

CANADA

A database of all the men who served in the Canadian Expeditionary Force can be found at www.archives.ca/02/020106_e.html, together with the scanned images of their attestation papers, which gives basic personal information. It is possible to order copies of full service records from the Personnel Records Unit, National Archives of Canada (NAC), 395 Wellington Street, Ottawa, Ontario K1A 0N3.

The NAC also has war diaries for Canadian units which are very similar to their British equivalents.

The Canadian Virtual War Museum, www.vac-acc.gc.ca/general/sub.cfm?source=collections/virtualmem, contains details of Canadians who died in the war and their last resting place. The information is very similar to that supplied by the Commonwealth War Graves Commission. In addition there are also pages about Canada during the First World War.

Scanned images from the Canadian Book of Remembrance, the original of which is housed in the Peace Tower on Parliament Hill, Ottawa, can be found at http://collections.ic.gc.ca/books/books.htm. It

Attestation papers for John ('Jack') Robert Fowler who enlisted in the 102nd Battalion, Canadian Expeditionary Force at Vancouver in January 1916 (National Archives of Canada reference RG150, Accession 1992–93/166, Box 3247-53). Jack Fowler survived the war.

Detail of a beaver found on the Vimy Ridge memorial to the Canadians who lost their lives during the war.

contains the names of 66,665 Canadians who died in the First World War (as well as in other conflicts). There is also a separate volume for Newfoundland.

The Canadian Military Heritage Project (www.rootsweb.com/~canmil/ancestor.htm) contains pages relating to Canada's role in the First World War including a useful page offering advice about tracing military ancestors.

INDIA

Indian forces initially fought on the Western Front, but during 1915 and 1916 were largely transferred to Mesopotamia (Iraq). Men also served at Gallipoli and in East Africa. Some 1.4m Indians served during the war largely commanded by British officers. Service and other records are split between Britain and India.

The Oriental and India Office Collections at the British Libarary has a number of records relating to the service of officers in the Indian Army, but no service records as such. There is also a biographical card index to British civil and military employees living in India: British Library, Oriental and India Office Collections, 96 Euston Rd, London, NW1 2DB (tel: 020 7412 7873; website: http://www.bl.uk/collections/orientalandindian.html).

The National Archives of India, New Delhi, 110011 (website: http://nationalarchives.nic.in) holds records of the Army Department, which may contain details about ordinary native soldiers who served in the Indian Army.

Indian Army officers who lost their lives during the war are described in S.B. and D.B. Jarvis, *The Cross of Sacrifice: Officers Who Died in the Service of the British, Indian and East African Regiments and Corps, 1914–1919* (Naval and Military Press, 1993).

At least 20% of British merchant seamen came from the Indian sub-continent and were generally referred to as 'lascars'. Records for them (as well as for the Chinese, Africans and seamen of other nationalities) who served on board British merchant ships are described in Chapter 4.

NEWFOUNDLAND

Until 1949 Newfoundland was separate from Canada and this is reflected in the records. However there were close links between the two countries, so researchers may need to try Canadian sources as well.

Surviving service records of the Newfoundland Regiment are with the Provincial Archives of Newfoundland and Labrador, Colonial Building, Military Road, St. John's, Newfoundland A1C 2C9 (website: www.gov.nf.ca/panl).

Unfortunately the website contains no further details of how these records are arranged or what they contain. The archives are due to move in Spring 2003 to new premises called The Rooms in St John's, which will be jointly shared with the provincial museum and art gallery (www.therooms.ca). A far from complete list of men who served in the Regiment during the war is at: http://ngb.chebucto.org/NFREG/Additions/additions.htm. An interesting on-line exhibition about Newfoundland's role during the war is at www.heritage.nf.ca/greatwar/default.html.

A number of Newfoundlanders enlisted in the Royal Naval Reserve and records of the Reserve are described in Chapter 4.

NEW ZEALAND

Personnel records of men who served in the New Zealand Expeditionary Force are held by the New Zealand Defence Force, Personnel Archives, Trentham Camp, Private Bag, Upper Hutt, New Zealand (website: www.army.mil.nz/nzarmy/). There is a charge for each service record ordered.

New Zealand's list of its citizens who died while serving in the armed forces during the Great War was published in 1924. Titled *New Zealand Expeditionary Force Roll of Honour*, it contains 16,697 names. The Roll was reprinted by the Naval and Military Press in 2002. An excellent website devoted to the history of New Zealand during the First World War can be found at www.greatwar.org.nz.

SOUTH AFRICA

Service records are held by: South African National Defence Force, Documentation Service, Private Bag X289, Pretoria 0001.

Because of the policies of the Union government black South Africans only served in non-combatant roles.

COLONIES

The majority of colonies were too small to do more than raise a local militia and send financial contributions to London. Only two colonial regiments saw any fighting, the King's African Rifles in German East Africa (Tanganyika/Tanzania) and the West India Regiment in Cameroon. The West India Regiment also later served on the Western Front but for racial reasons did not see any fighting and was engaged on labour duties. Service records and other records should be found as for other British units. Officers of the King's African Rifles and other units raised in East Africa are described in S.B. and D.B. Jarvis, *The Cross of Sacrifice: Officers Who Died in the Service of the British, Indian and East African Regiments and Corps, 1914–1919* (Naval and Military Press, 1993). A website on the experiences of the West India Regiment can be found at http://website.lineone.net/~bwir/ bwi_regt.htm.

NON-IMPERIAL FORCES

Researching the war efforts of countries outside the British Empire presents peculiar difficulties. The organisation of forces during the war and the current arrangement of the records may seem baffling. It can be particularly difficult if you are conducting research by post or e-mail as most archives are not geared up to dealing with genealogical researchers, so expect many frustrating weeks waiting for unhelpful replies. The Lithuanian Archives, for example, now regularly take a year or so to reply to genealogical enquiries. It certainly helps if you can correspond in the language of the country in which you are interested. It also helps to do your reading beforehand, so that you can ask questions that you know can be answered by the archive, and, particularly, that you know with which unit the person you are interested in served. The Imperial War Museum may well have books that can help your research. It is also worth contacting your local LDS Church family history centre to see whether they can obtain microfilms for you, as the Church has large collections of genealogical material from around the world. More information about this material can be found at www.familysearch.org.

BELGIUM

Britain went to war to protect 'gallant little Belgium' and much of the fighting on the Western Front took part in the extreme west of the country. Most of Belgium was under German occupation, and the people endured four years of hardship, being prevented from starvation only by massive relief efforts organised by the American engineer Herbert Hoover. Their experience is told at the In Flanders Fields Museum in Ypres.

Service records for both officers and other ranks are held by the Royal Museum of the Army and Military History, Jubelpark 3, 1000 Brussels (website: www.klm-mra.be). The Museum's archives also have a great deal of additional information about the Belgian army.

A website (in Flemish) containing details of the location of the graves of Belgian soldiers who lost their lives during the war (including details of graveyards in Britain) can be found at: www.geocities.com/ Pentagon/Camp/4403/.

Over 160,000 Belgian civilian refugees came to Britain during the First World War and were looked after largely by local voluntary organisations under the auspices of the War Refugees Committee. Cards about individual refugees, together with correspondence about their care, are held at the National Archives in series MH 8. There may also be some material at local record offices.

FRANCE

For the first three years the French were the major partner within the Allies, blunting the German advance during the autumn of 1914 and then during 1916 enduring the worst horrors of the war as their forces defended the fortress city of Verdun against a vicious onslaught. Conditions for the ordinary French soldier, however, were poor and coupled with poor leadership which saw thousands of lives lost unnecessarily in pointless attacks on German lines, led to a widespread mutiny in the spring of 1917. The mutiny was eventually suppressed without, remarkably, the Germans ever finding out. Thereafter, however, the French no longer played a leading role in the fighting, although Marshal Foch was appointed Allied supreme commander in March 1918.

Access to military records is restricted for 120 years from the soldier's birth and they are available only to the veteran or next of kin. However, operational files and conscription papers are now largely open. You will need to contact: Service historique de l'Armée de Terre, Vieux Fort, Chateau de Vincennes, 94304 Vincennes Cedex.

Some French army records, including medal records and pension records, are at: Bureau centrale des Archives administrives militaries à Pau, Caserene Bernadotte, 64000 Pau.

Graves and memorials to French men who lost their lives during the war are maintained by: Ministère des Anciens Combattants et Victimes de Guerre, 139 rue de Bercy, 75012 Paris.

The French Army Museum has extensive galleries devoted to the First World War and France's part in it, at Musée de l'Armée, Hôtel National des Invalides, 129 rue de Grenelle, 75700 Paris 07 SP (website: www.invalides.org/invalidesgb).

French troops in the trenches 'somewhere in France'. Until mid-1916 they bore most of the fighting on the Western Front.

Memorial to French soldiers who lost their lives defending the town of Ypres.

GERMANY

Germany attacked France and Russia simultaneously in July and August 1914 and hoped to knock one or other out, but although success was within grasp in France the plan failed. The reasons behind the attack have long been debated. For four years she (with fairly minimal help from her allies, Austria-Hungary, Bulgaria and Turkey) managed to defend her gains on the Western Front and force the Russians out of the war. Operation Michael (the German Spring Offensive) in March 1918 pushed the British nearly back to the sea. It ground to a halt by May, in part because the German troops looted Allied supply dumps and became too drunk on the alcohol they found there to advance further. This was a sign of increasing war weariness, coupled with food shortages at home, which led to a collapse in morale in the armed forces in the autumn of 1918 and the signing of the Armistice on 11th November.

Germany in 1914 was a federation of different states. By far the most important was Prussia, whose army included those of the smaller duchies and principalities. However, Bavaria and Saxony also maintained separate armies. Most Prussian records were destroyed by bombing in April 1945. Surviving records (including those for the German Navy which survived) are with the Federal Archives Military Section, Wiesentalstrasse 10, 79115 Freiburg-in-Breisgau (website: www.bundesarchiv.de/standorte2.php?SID=4).

Bavarian Army records (including service records) are with the Bavarian War Archives, Leonrodstr 57, Postfach 22152, 80636 Munich. And, for Saxony, at Saxon Archives, Archivstr 14, 01097 Dresden.

The German equivalent of the CWGC is the Volksbund Deutsche Kriegsgräberfürsorge e.V. It can be contacted at: Bundesgeschäftsstelle, Werner-Hilpert-Straße 2, 34112 Kassel (website: www.volksbund.de).

Its website (in German) describes the work of the Volksbund, and contains details of German cemeteries around the world. There is also a searchable database to the war dead, although information is posted to you, rather than directly available on-line.

An interesting website describing general genealogical research in Germany is www.genealogienetz.de. A simple introduction to German genealogy is Peter Towey, *Tracing Your German Ancestors* (2nd Edition, Federation of Family History Societies, 2002).

RUSSIA

The fighting on the Eastern Front was far more fluid than in the West. After an initial advance by the Russians, they were pushed further back into Russia itself. Conditions for the troops were often appalling – far worse than anything experienced on the Western Front – and in addition they were poorly led and equipped. It is little wonder that when revolution broke out in Petrograd in 1917 it quickly spread to the Army. A separate peace was signed with Germany at Brest-Litovsk in early 1918.

Service records for officers and men, together with other information about the Russian forces during the war, are held by the Russian State Military Historical Archive, 2 Baumanskaya, 3, 107864 Moscow.

An excellent English language website devoted to researching Russian roots is at www.mtu-net.ru/rrr.

UNITED STATES

The Americans only entered the war in April 1917, after the Germans had begun to indiscriminately sink American ships crossing the Atlantic. However, the US had been supplying vast amounts of munitions and machine tools to the Allies for several years previously. A number of Americans had already enlisted in mainly Canadian units, although an ambulance unit and air squadron of American volunteers were attached to the French. The build up of men in France proceeded very slowly and it wasn't until May 1918 that American troops began to take a large part in the fighting. Unfortunately, General Pershing, the American commander, refused to adopt the tactics of his Allies, learnt after four years of bitter experience, so US losses were heavier than they should have been.

Some 80% of service records for soldiers (both officers and enlisted men) were destroyed in a disastrous fire in 1973, although naval personnel records survive. They are with: National Personnel Records Center, Military Records Facility, 9700 Page Ave, St Louis, MO 63132-5100 (website:www.archives.gov/facilities/mo/st_louis/-military_personnel_records.html).

There are other sources, however, which could provide information about Doughboy ancestors. One of the most important are draft registration cards, which provide personal details of men who registered to serve (although not everybody was called up). These cards have been filmed and are widely available at state archives as well as at the regional facilities of the (American) National Archives (NARA). NARA also has war diaries, naval, merchant marine, military and aviation records (including some personnel records): National Archives and Records Administration, 700 Pennsylvania Avenue, Washington, DC, 20408 (website: www.archives.gov). An on-line database devoted to men from Missouri who served in the US Army and Navy is at www.sos.state.mo.us/archives/wwl/default.asp.

Battlefield cemeteries and memorials are cared for by the American Battlefields Monuments Commission, Casimir Pulaski Building, 20 Massachusetts Ave NW, Washington, DC, 20314-0300 (website: www.abmc.gov). The website contains an on-line database which allows you to find where an individual is buried, together with brief personal information.

The American equivalent to the Western Front Association is the: Great War Society, BOX 18585, Stanford, CA, 94309. The website: www.worldwar1.com/tgws/tgws2.htm is devoted to the study of the First World War and America's role in it.

Appendix I

LIST OF USEFUL ADDRESSES

&

Listed below are addresses (and very brief summaries of their holdings of First World War material) of archives, museums and other places which you might need to visit in the course of your research. Before you set out it is a very good idea to ring up (or send an e-mail) to make sure that they have what you are looking for and indeed that they are open. Unless otherwise indicated you will need to make an appointment to see particular records. And don't forget to take a pencil and notepad.

NATIONAL ARCHIVES AND LIBRARIES

British Library
96 Euston Rd
London NW1 2DB
Tel: 020 7412 7000
Website: www.bl.uk
The British Library is Britain's national library. It has copies of virtually every book published in the UK, together with private papers of statesmen and other important figures. If you are interested in Indian troops on the Western Front or the campaign in Mesopotamia you might need to use the India Office and Oriental Collections (IOOC), which house the records of the India Office and other material such as Indian Soldiers Comfort Fund. Catalogues of some of the IOOC material can be found on the Access to Archives website, including lists of British people who joined the Indian Army and Navy (www.a2a.pro.gov.uk).

To get access to the library you will need to apply for a reader's ticket and demonstrate why you need to use the library's collections. There is no need to make an appointment, although you should allow plenty of time to get your reader's ticket.

The library catalogue is available on-line (www.blpc.bl.uk). As it includes the vast majority of books published in the British Isles, it is an important resource, especially if you are checking what books were published about your area or subject of interest.

British Library Newspaper Library
Colindale
London NW9 5HE
Tel: 020 7412 7353
Website: www.bl.uk/collections/newspapers.html
The British Library Newspaper Library, which is almost opposite Colindale underground station, houses the UK's largest and most comprehensive collections of newspapers and magazines, some published during the First World War (but seemingly not trench newspapers). You will need a reader's ticket, although main BL passes are also valid. A catalogue to its holdings is available on-line. Again there is no need to make an appointment.

Family Records Centre
1 Myddleton St
London EC1R 1UW
Tel: 020 8392 5300
Website: www.familyrecords.gov.uk
The Family Records Centre is a joint venture between the National Archives and the Office for National Statistics. On the ground floor you can find indexes to the men who died during the First World War and order their death certificates (although they probably won't add anything to the information you already have). Certificates cost £7 each (2003 price) or you can order them by post for £11.50 from the General Register Office on 0870 243 7788, provide you have the full GRO reference. Under government proposals to reform the civil registration system, an absurd restriction may be placed on access to death certificates less than a hundred years old, so you should obtain your certificates now.

The indexes for army officers and other ranks indicate the regiment, rank and service number. The Marine Death indexes (Royal Navy as well as Merchant Marine) contain the name of the ship and the age of the deceased. There is also a slim volume of Indian Army deaths. Also of interest are chaplain's returns which record births, marriages and deaths at bases in Britain and overseas. There is no need to make an appointment or acquire a reader's ticket.

On the first floor can be found the census records, including those for 1901 both on-line (visit www.census.pro.gov.uk) or on microfiche. Almost everybody who served in British forces during the war can be found in the 1901 census (except the author's paternal grandfather who irritatingly seems to have been raised on a Malayan rubber plantation, so doesn't appear there).

House of Lords Record Office (sometimes called the Parliamentary Archives)
House of Lords
London SW1A 0PW
Tel: 020 7219 3074
Website: www.parliament.uk
The Record Office holds the archives of Parliament and also has the papers of a number of prominent politicians, including Lloyd George and Lord Beaverbrook. Indexes to many of their holdings can be found on the Access to Archives website (www.a2a.pro.gov.uk).

Liddle Collection
Special Collections
The Brotherton Library
University of Leeds
Leeds LS2 9JT
Tel: 0113 343 5518
Website: www.leeds.ac.uk/library/spcoll/liddle
The Liddle Collection is a major collection of private papers and other material relating to the two world wars. Details of its holdings can be found on-line.

Public Record Office
See National Archives

National Register of Archives
Quality House
Quality Court
Chancery Lane
London WC2A 1HP
Tel: 020 7242 1198
Website: www.hmc.gov.uk

The National Register of Archives holds copies of listings of collections supplied by local record offices in England and Wales. Its indexes can be searched on-line. They also have catalogues for many records at local record offices that can be consulted in their welcoming reading room. No appointment is necessary. In April 2003 the HMC merged with the Public Record Office to form the National Archives and the reading room will be transferred to Kew by the end of 2003.

National Archives
Ruskin Ave
Kew, Richmond
Surrey TW9 4DU
Tel: 020 8392 5200
Website:www.pro.gov.uk
The National Archives (NA, formerly the Public Record Office) is the national archives of the United Kingdom and England. It has major collections of material relating to the First World War, which are fully described elsewhere in this book, and in Ian F.W. Beckett, *The Essential Guide to Sources in the National Archives* (PRO, 2002). Its catalogue is

The outside of the National Archives (Public Record Office) building at Kew, which houses most of the official records relating to the First World War.

The reading room at the National Archives where you can study some of the most important documents relating to the First World War. (National Archives)

on-line, and you can also download leaflets about the records from the website www.pro.gov.uk.

To get access to this material you will need a reader's ticket, which will be issued on your first visit. There is no need to make an appointment. You will need to bring some form of identity with you. The NA is a huge place and can be very confusing to first-time visitors. After getting your ticket, it is a very good idea to go on one of the regular orientation tours that show you how to find references and order documents.

There are several reading rooms on the first floor for documents, microfilm and microfiche, and (on the second floor) maps and large documents. Also on the first floor is the Research Enquiries Room (RER) which has numerous catalogues and card indexes, and where you can ask the friendly and knowledgeable staff about your research.

There is also a shop with an excellent range of books about the war, a restaurant and an internet café. A small museum displays treasures from the Archives' holdings, often including a few items from the First World War.

Society of Genealogists
14 Charterhouse Buildings
Goswell Road
London EC1M 7BA
Tel: 020 7251 8799
Website: www.sog.org.uk
The Society's library provides a major resource for family historians, with much material that may not easily be found elsewhere. Holdings for the First World War include sizeable collections of regimental histories, Army and Navy Lists, together with other books, including several volumes of the *National Roll of Honour* and an extremely rare book on the British community in Argentina during the war. They have a good range of CD-ROMs (including *Soldiers Died* and *The National Roll of Honour*) and free access to the large number of databases on the ancestry.com website. Non-members pay a fee to use the library: the 2003 rate was £3.30 per hour or £13.20 a day.

NATIONAL MUSEUMS

Fleet Air Arm Museum
RNAS
Yeovilton
Ilchester BA22 8HT
Tel: 01935 840565
Website: www.fleetairarm.com
The Museum has displays about the RNAS during the First World War. In addition the Research and Reference Centre has enlistment books for Naval and Royal Marine recruits, RNAS squadron line books (roughly equivalent to Operation Record Books), photographs and maps, as well as information about individual men who served with the Service and the subsequent Fleet Air Arm.

Imperial War Museum
Lambeth Road
London SE1 6HZ
Tel: 020 7416 5000
Website: www.iwm.org.uk
After the National Archives, the Imperial War Museum is the most important source for the First World War, ranging from artefacts to photographs and films, via books and documents. The Museum was established in 1917 specifically to collect material about the war – one of the earliest projects was the Women's War Work Collection to document women's contribution to the war effort. The major departments are Documents (with collections of private papers of all ranks from Private to Field Marshal), Photographs (40,000 images taken by official photographers), and Printed Books (books relating to all aspects of the war in Britain and elsewhere).

Anybody is welcome to use the research collections, although you must book an appointment at least a day in advance. The holdings are described in a free leaflet, *The Collections: An Access Guide*, which can be picked up at the Museum or requested by phone. It is also available on-line. The website also includes information about using the Museum for family history.

Catalogues to many of its holdings can be found on-line, although it has to be said that they are not easy to use.

The Museum is also home to the British National Inventory of War Memorials which records the existence of all war memorials. There are an estimated 55,000 such memorials for the First World War.

Among the many exhibits from the Great War on display in the Museum proper is a recreation of a trench. There is also an excellent bookshop and a café. There are no research facilities at either the Museum's branch at Duxford or the new IWM North in Manchester.

National Army Museum
Royal Hospital Road
London SW3 4HT
Tel. 020 7730 0717
Website: www.national-army-museum.ac.uk
The Museum has major collections relating to the British Army during the First World War, including regimental histories and magazines, *Army Lists*, photographs, and records of the Irish regiments which were disbanded on the creation of the Irish Free State in the early 1920s. Unfortunately getting access to the reading room is a bureaucratic

nightmare. Indexes to some holdings are now on the Access to Archives website (www.a2a.pro.gov.uk). There is a bookshop and café.

National Maritime Museum
Greenwich
London SE10 9NF
Tel: 020 8858 4422
Website: www.nmm.ac.uk
The Museum's library and archives hold the largest collection of material relating to Britain's maritime history in the world. The library's catalogue is on-line.

RAF Museum
Graham Park Way
London NW9 5LL
Tel: 020 8205 2266
Website: www.rafmuseum.org.uk
The Museum's library and archives hold substantial material about the history of aviation and the RAF and RFC in particular. Of especial interest in the archives are First World War casualty cards and record cards for individual aircraft, personal papers of former airmen, and some company records. In the library can be found aviation magazines (particularly *Flight*), which contain information about early aviators, and official air publications including training posters from the war. There are also extensive collections of photographs.

Royal Marines Museum
Eastney Barracks
Southsea
PO4 9PX
Tel: 01705 819385
Website: www.royalmarinesmuseum.co.uk.
Has some records about the Royal Marines and their wartime service.

Royal Naval Museum
HM Naval Base (PP66)
Portsmouth PO1 3NH
Tel: 023 9272 7562
Website: www.royalnavalmuseum.org.uk
Has some personnel papers of commanders and collections relating to

the WRNS, reference books include *Navy Lists* and *Jane's Naval Ships*.

Regimental museums

Almost every regiment has a museum, which displays its history and regimental memorabilia such as the silver used in the officers' mess or trophies captured from the enemy. Attached to these museums are often regimental record offices, which may have records about individual officers or soldiers, collections of photographs and printed ephemera including regimental journals. However, their holdings vary dramatically. The Essex Regiment Museum, for example, has almost no official records, although they have a useful database of material built up over many years about individuals who served with the regiment. The records in general are described in Norman Holding, *The Location of British Army Records, 1914–1918* (4th edition, Federation of Family History Societies, 1999). All regimental museums, addresses, opening hours are given in Terence and Shirley Wise, *A Guide to Military Museums and Other Places of Military Interest* (10th edition, Terence Wise, 2001). Similar information can be found on the web at www.armymuseums.org.uk.

OTHER

Commonwealth War Graves Commission

2 Marlow Rd
Maidenhead SL6 7DX
Tel: 01628 34221
Website: www.cwgc.org
The Commission looks after over a million war graves of British and Commonwealth service personnel who lost their lives in the two world

wars in 150 countries worldwide from Albania to Zimbabwe. Brief details of each individual are listed in the Debt of Honour register, together with where they are buried or commemorated, which may be searched on-line or you can ring or write for details of any individual in whom you are interested.

Guildhall Library (Manuscripts Department)
Aldermanbury
London EC2P 2EJ
Tel: 020 7332 1863
Website: www.ihrinfo.ac.uk/gh
The Guildhall Library has considerable amounts of material about the City of London and the businesses that flourished there. Of particular interest is the Lloyd's Marine Collection which contains much about merchant shipping during the war. It also holds records of the London livery companies.

Family History Centres
Hyde Park Family History Centre
64-68 Exhibition Rd
London SW7 2PA
Tel: 020 7589 8561
Website: www.familysearch.org
The LDS Church (the Mormons) runs a network of family history centres across Britain, of which the Hyde Park Centre is the largest. At these centres it is possible to order microfilms from the Family History Library in Salt Lake City (by far the largest genealogical library in the world) for a few pence. Although the Church is primarily interested in filming records to do with baptism and marriage, they have filmed many service records and other material. In particular they have a set of the films of the British 'burnt' and 'unburnt' service records. Non-Mormons are very welcome to use these facilities. The Hyde Park Centre can tell you which is your nearest centre.

The logo of the Western Front Association, Britain's society for the study of the First World War. If you become fascinated by the 'war to end wars' it is well worth joining. (Western Front Association)

SOCIETIES

Western Front Association
Paul Hanson
Membership Secretary
17 Aldrin Way
Cannon Park
Coventry CV4 7DP
Website: www.westernfrontassociation.com
Britain's foremost society for the study of the First World War, particularly the Western Front. Members receive *Stand To!*, an informative membership bulletin and the opportunity to attend seminars and events organised by local branches. Membership (2003 rate) is £20 pa.

Cross and Cockcade International
Membership Secretary
5 Cave Down
Bristol BS16 2TL
Website: www.crossandcockade.com
Researches and publishes information on all aspects of the First World War in the air. The Society is probably best known for its journal *Cross and Cockcade International*, published quarterly.

Friends of War Memorials
4 Lower Belgrave Street
London SW1W 0LA
Website: www.war-memorials.com
Exists to protect and preserve war memorials and to educate the public
as to their value and importance.

Great War Society
13 Ashburton Rd,
Wesbury on Trim BS10 5QN
www.thegreatwarsociety.co.uk
One of several re-enactment groups specialising in the period.

Appendix II

BATTLEFIELD TOURISM

❧

Almost as soon as the armistice was signed tourists began to visit the shattered villages and the battlefields of the Western Front. Between the wars the British Legion organised pilgrimages for the families of those who had fallen and so that old comrades could visit the places they had spent their youth. The old sites of France and Flanders remain popular destinations, particularly with British visitors. Indeed, if you have any interest in the First World War you should try to visit the sites of the great battles and the memorials they left behind. On the whole there isn't much to see on the ground, as the scars of war have all but healed, however the cemeteries and the great memorials are very moving. There are also several excellent museums. You won't regret a visit.

Numerous tour operators run regular trips to the battlefields (including those at Gallipoli and outside Europe). Tours are geared either for first time visitors or perhaps to examine particular battles or other aspects of the war. Included in the fare are the accommodation, meals, coach travel and the services of an expert guide. Provided they have advanced notice, most are only too happy to detour to a particular cemetery so that you can visit an individual grave. A three-day introductory trip to France and Flanders costs in the region of £400 per person. Three of the most reputable operators are:

Holts Battlefield Tours, The Plough, High Street, Eastry, Sandwich, Kent CT13 0HF, tel: 01304 612248 *www.battletours.co.uk*

Flanders Tours, PO Box 240, Ellington, Huntingdon PE28 0YE, tel: 01480 890966, *www.flanderstours.co.uk*

Tours with Experts (operated in conjunction with the Imperial War Museum), Red Lion Building, 9 Liverpool Road North, Maghull L31 2HB, tel: 0151 520 1290 *www.iwm.org.uk/tours* or *www.tours-with-experts.com*

It is perfectly possible to tour the Western Front, however, under your own steam. You can easily travel by car from central London to the market place at Ypres in five hours (back in 1916 it took at least eighteen), so a day trip to the Salient is possible. Indeed, I've done it. Roads in the area are excellent and there are motorway links both to Flanders and to the Somme from Calais. Unfortunately it is not a journey you can so easily do by public transport, although Ypres and Poperinge are on a railway branch line from Courtrai (Kortrijk), and Amiens and Arras are served by French railways.

There are a number of guidebooks covering the battlefields in varying degrees of detail. One that covers the whole area is Rose E. Coombs, *Before Endeavours Fade: A Guide to the Battlefields of the First World War* (After the Battle, 1994). Another comprehensive guide is Tonie and Valmai Holt, *Major & Mrs Holt's Battlefield Guide to World War One Battles* (3rd edition, Pen and Sword, 2003). Pen and Sword also publish a series of more detailed guides in their excellent 'Battlefield Europe' series. Richard Holmes, *War Walks* (BBC, 1997) is a guide to six battlefields of northern France and Belgium, including Mons and Le Cateau, the Somme, and Arras. In the early 1990s the Canadian journalist Stephen O'Shea walked the whole of the Western Front from the Belgian coast to the Swiss border and his account *Back to the Front: An Accidental Historian Walks the Trenches of World War I* (Robson, 1997) is worth reading, although his grasp of the history of the period is pretty shaky! A website offering useful advice to people wishing to visit the battlefields can be found at: http://battlefields1418.50megs.com/main_menu.htm.

The French map company Michelin has produced two modern road maps of the areas with the densest concentration of war cemeteries in northern France and Belgium. The maps in Michelin's 1:200,000 series (Nos 51 and 52) are overprinted with the exact location of each cemetery and memorial and are indexed. They cost £3 (2003) each and can be obtained from the Commonwealth War Graves Commission.

The most important sites, which you should probably include in any visit to the battlefields, are:

SOMME

MUSEUMS

Historial de la Grand Guerre, Chateau de Peronne, F-80201 Peronne, tel: (0033) 322 831418, www. historial.org. The superb Historial is the

The Harvest of Death

Every year farmers plough up unexploded shells, bullets and barbed wire, which can often be seen in piles by the side of the road waiting to be taken away by the French and Belgian armies. For good reason this is known as the 'harvest of death' and even after 90 years remains extremely dangerous. However tempting it might be, please do not pick up any of these items. A friend of mine was hospitalised for months with mustard gas poisoning after touching a shell for a few seconds.

Examining munitions dug up on the Somme.

major museum for the area with extensive displays and exhibitions (in English as well as French) on all aspects of the First World War. There is an admission charge.

Musée Somme, The Ramparts, F.80203 Albert, tel: (0033) 322 755 37, www.somme-1916.org. The Musée is based in a Second World War underground shelter in the centre of the town with numerous displays about the battle and its aftermath. Admission €3.50 adults, €2 children.

BATTLEFIELD REMNANTS

Lochnagar Crater (La Boiselle) is the only surviving site of the 17 mines which were exploded under the German lines at the time of the British advance in July 1916.

Beaumont Hamel Memorial Park (Beaumont Hamel) is dedicated to the memory of men of the Newfoundland Regiment who fought and died here on 1st July 1916. In less than thirty minutes, 710 of the 776 men who had left the trenches had been killed, wounded or reported missing: probably the greatest loss of any unit on the day. The site still contains the trenches, shell holes and twisted remains of 'Danger Tree', which were left after the Armistice, although after 85 years they are little more than hollows in the ground. The site is dominated by a giant caribou: the emblem of the Newfoundland Regiment.

MONUMENTS

Delville Wood, which South African battalions attempted to take in late July 1916. It was the site of some of the bloodiest fighting of the war. It now houses the moving South African National War Memorial.

The Thiepval Anglo-French Memorial dominates much of the local skyline. It commemorates the 73,000 British men who fell on the Somme between July 1915 and March 1918, and who have no known grave. Sir Edward Lutyens designed the 141 foot tall monument, which was unveiled in 1932. There is an appeal at present to raise money to build a visitors' centre.

Ulster Tower, near Thiepval, commemorates the men of the Ulster Division who died on 1 July. The memorial is a replica of Helen's

The Anglo-French Memorial at Thiepval on the Somme carries the names of 73,000 British and Commonwealth men who have no known grave. At 141 feet (45m) tall it can be seen for miles across the battlefield

Tower, a well-known Northern Ireland landmark. It is now dedicated to improving relationships between the two communities in the province. For more information contact the Somme Heritage Centre, Whitespots County Park, 233 Bangor Rd, Newtownards BT23 7PH, or visit www.irishsoldier.org.

Serre Road Cemeteries, near Auchonvilliers. These three cemeteries contain the bodies of nearly 20,000 men who died during the battle. French, German and British graves are found here. There are numerous other cemeteries nearby which testify to the great losses during the battle.

YPRES SALIENT

There is a useful (if frustratingly incomplete) website which contains much information about battlefield tourism around Ypres: www.greatwar.be.

MUSEUMS

In Flanders Fields, Lakenhalle, Grote Markt 34, B-8000 Ypres, tel: (0032) 57 228584, www.inflandersfields.be (there is an admission charge). An award winning museum in the restored Lace Hall looking at the experience of soldiers in the Salient and the civilians whose lives were dramatically altered by the war.

BATTLEFIELD REMNANTS

Sanctuary Wood, Menin Road (south east of Ypres). One of the strangest places to visit on the whole of the Western Front: part locals' bar, part museum and, frankly, part freak show. Most people come to visit the now almost entirely eroded remains of the trenches in the wood behind the museum. There is a good range of artefacts which have been dug up locally on display. Many of the museum exhibits, however, are not for the squeamish. There is an admission charge.

Talbot House (Poperinghe). Strictly not a battlefield, but a building that housed a unique social club for officers and other ranks run by the Revd Tubby Clayton during the war (and which led to the Toc H movement). The premises have been sensitively restored to how they looked during the war. The history of the House and Clayton himself is told in Paul Chapman, *A Haven in Hell* (Pen and Sword, 2000).

MONUMENTS

Langemarck German Cemetery (Langemarck) is the only German cemetery on the Salient, the resting place of 44,292 bodies in mass graves. The sombre black tombstones and the general arrangement provide a chilling reminder that the enemy too suffered enormous losses during the war.

Menin Gate (Ypres). A few metres from the Grote Markt is the memorial to the British and Empire men who lost their lives in the Salient and have no known grave. Nearly 55,000 soldiers who died between October 1914 and 15 August 1917 are commemorated here. The 35,000 men who died subsequently are commemorated at Tyne Cot Cemetery. Designed by Sir Reginald Blomfield, it was unveiled in July 1927 by Field Marshal Lord Plumer. If you are in Ypres overnight it is

There's a perceptible sense of foreboding at the German cemetery at Langemarck near Ypres. The remains of soldiers from all over the Salient are buried here.

worth attending the ceremony that takes place at 8 pm each evening, where buglers from the local fire brigade play the Last Post.

Tyne Cot Cemetery (near Zonnebeke). The largest British war cemetery with 12,000 graves (including 1,350 Australian, 1,000 Canadian and 500 New Zealander).

ELSEWHERE

Vimy Ridge (between Arras and Lens) is the principal Canadian monument on the Western Front and commemorates a successful Allied assault on German lines. As well as the very impressive memorial which dominates the local skyline (and look out for the miniature beavers!), there are preserved trenches, a tunnel system and a visitors' centre.

Appendix III

THE FIRST WORLD WAR IN STATISTICS

❦

It is notoriously difficult to find accurate statistics, even basic information about the numbers of men who served in the war, were killed, wounded or taken prisoner. In some cases, statistics were never kept, in others figures were conflated (perhaps including civilians or servicewomen), or exaggerated by authors for their own purposes. I believe the ones given below to be reasonably accurate.

	Men mobilised	Killed	Wounded	Prisoners of war
Austria-Hungary	7,800,000	1,200,000	3,620,000	2,200,000
Belgium	267,000	13,716	44,686	34,659
British Empire	8,904,467	908,371	2,090,212	191,652
Bulgaria	1,200,000	87,500	152,390	27,029
France	8,410,000	1,375,800	4,266,000	537,000
Germany	11,000,000	1,773,700	4,216,058	1,152,800
Greece	230,000	5,000	21,000	1,000
Italy	5,615,000	650,000	947,000	600,000
Japan	800,000	300	907	3
Montenegro	50,000	3,000	10,000	7,000
Portugal	100,000	7,222	13,751	12,318
Romania	750,000	335,706	120,000	80,000
Russia	12,000,000	1,700,000	4,950,000	2,500,000
Serbia	707,343	45,000	133,148	152,958
Turkey	2,850,000	325,000	400,000	250,000
United States	4,355,000	126,000	234,300	4,526

Source: figures correlated from tables on Trenches on the Web website (www.worldwar1.com/tlcrates.htm) and Spartacus Schoolnet (www.spartacus.schoolnet.co.uk/fwwdeaths.htm). Another set of figures, however, can be found in Niall Ferguson, *The Pity of War* (Penguin, 1998), pp295, 298.

Population and recruiting for the British Army

	Total enlisted	% of total population	% of male population
United Kingdom	4,970,902	11	22
England	4,006,158	12	24
Scotland	557,618	12	24
Wales	272,924	11	22
Ireland	134,202	3	6
Australia	331,814		13
Canada	458,814		13
Newfoundland	6,173		Not given
New Zealand	112,228		19
South Africa	76,184		11
India	Not given		
Colonies	Not given		

Source: *Statistics of the Military Effort of the British Empire During the Great War* (War Office, 1922, reprinted Naval and Military Press, 1999), p363. Dominion figures are for 'total number of men sent overseas or under growing training as at 1 November 1918'.

Numbers of volunteers and conscripts enlisted in the British Army August 1914–November 1918

	Total number	% of total
Volunteers	2,466,719	49.6
Conscripts	2,504,183	50.4
TOTAL	4,970,902	

Source: Ilana R. Bet-El, *Conscripts: Lost Legions of the Great War* (Sutton Publishing, 1999), pp2, 13.

Approximate number of British and Empire casualties from 4 August 1914 to 31 December 1920: deaths (killed in action, died of wounds, missing, died of wounds while a prisoner of war)

	Officers	Other ranks	TOTAL
United Kingdom	37,452	664,958	702,410
Australia	2,862	56,468	59,330
Canada	2,887	53,752	56,639
Newfoundland	54	1,150	1,204
New Zealand	735	15,976	16,711
South Africa	336	6,785	7,121
India	2,286	62,163	64,449
Colonies	91	416	507
TOTAL	46,703	861,668	908,371

Source: *Statistics of the Military Effort of the British Empire During the Great War* (War Office, 1922, reprinted Naval and Military Press, 1999), p237.

Approximate number of British and Empire casualties from 4 August 1914 to 31 December 1920: wounded

	Officers	Other ranks	TOTAL
United Kingdom	79,445	1,583,180	1,662,625
Australia	6,304	145,867	152,171
Canada	6,347	143,385	149,732
Newfoundland	65	2,249	2,314
New Zealand	1,724	39,593	41,317
South Africa	569	11,460	12,029
Indian	3,413	65,801	69,214
Colonies	158	652	810
TOTAL	98,025	1,992,187	2,090,212

Source: *Statistics of the Military Effort of the British Empire During the Great War* (War Office, 1922, reprinted Naval and Military Press, 1999), p237.

Approximate number of British and Empire casualties from 4 August 1914 to 31 December 1920: prisoners of war

	Officers	Other ranks	TOTAL
United Kingdom	6,482	163,907	170,389
Australia	173	3,911	4,084
Canada	236	3,493	3,729
Newfoundland	6	144	150
New Zealand	10	488	498
South Africa	70	1,468	1,538
Indian	430	10,864	11,264
Colonies	0	0	0
TOTAL	7,407	184,245	191,652

Source: *Statistics of the Military Effort of the British Empire During the Great War* (War Office, 1922, reprinted Naval and Military Press, 1999), p237.

Total expenditure 1914–1918 (millions of dollars)

	Germany	Britain	France	Russia	Italy	USA
1914–15	2,920	2,493	1,994	1,239	979	761
1915–16	5,836	7,195	3,827	1,180	1,632	742
1916–17	5,609	10,303	6,277	4,585	2,524	2,086
1917–18	8,579	12,704	7,794	2,774	3,012	13,791
1918–19	9,445	12,611	10,116	-	4,744	18,351
TOTAL	32,388	45,307	30,009	11,778	12,892	35,731

Source: Ferguson, *The Pity of War*, p323. As Ferguson notes: 'The most striking point of all about the First World War is that it cost much more – roughly twice as much – to win it than lose it.'

A series of statistics about the war can also be found on the web at: www.spartacus.schoolnet.co.uk/FWWstatistics.htm

Appendix IV

FURTHER READING

✤

Essential reference books

Ian F.W. Beckett, *The First World War: The Essential Guide to Sources in the National Archives* (PRO Publications, 2002)

David Borrill, *Great War Family Ancestry Resource Booklet* (available from the author 21 Galfrid Rd, Bilton, Hull HU11 4EJ)

Philip J. Haythornthwaite, *The World War One Source Book* (Arms and Armour, 1992)

John Laffin, *Western Front Companion 1914–1918: A–Z Source to the Battles, Weapons, People, Places, Air Combat* (Sutton Publishing, 1997)

Terence and Shirley Wise, *A Guide to Military Museums and Other Places of Military Interest* (10th edition, Terence Wise, 2001)

Statistics of the Military Effort of the British Empire During the Great War (War Office, 1922, reprinted Naval and Military Press, 1999)

General reference books

Janet Foster and Julia Sheppard, *British Archives: A Guide to Archive Resources in the United Kingdom* (4th edition, Macmillan, 2001)

Jeremy Gibson and Pamela Peskett, *Record Offices and How to Find Them* (8th edition, Federation of Family History Societies, 2002)

Family history reference books

Simon Fowler, *The Joy of Family History* (PRO Publications, 2001)

Mark Herber, *Ancestral Trails: The Complete Guide to British Family History and Genealogy* (Sutton Publishing, 1997)

Christina K. Schaefer, *The Great War: A Guide to the Service Records of All the World's Fighting Men and Volunteers* (Genealogical Publishing Company, 1998)

In addition both the National Archives and the Imperial War Museum publish free leaflets on aspects of their records relating to genealogy and the First World War. They are available on-line or by ringing the institutions (see Appendix I for details). Similar leaflets for the Army have also been prepared by the Army Museums Ogilby Trust at www.armymuseums.org.uk.

General histories of the war

As might be expected there are large numbers of general introductions to the war. Here is a selection of recent books:

Ian F.W. Beckett, *The Great War 1914–1918* (Longman, 2001)

Hugh Cecil and Peter H. Liddle (ed), *Facing Armageddon: The First World War Experienced* (Leo Cooper, 1996). A collection of essays about aspects of the war.

Niall Ferguson, *The Pity of war* (Penguin, 1998). Offers a controversial reassessment of the war and how it was fought.

Richard Holmes, *The Western Front* (BBC Consumer Publishing, 2001)

John Keegan, *The First World War* (Pimlico, 1999). Probably the best modern account.

Gary Sheffield, *Forgotten Victory: The First World War: Myths and Realities* (Headline, 2001)

Hew Strachan (ed), *The Oxford Illustrated History of the First World War* (Oxford UP, 1998)

Hew Strachan, *The First World War: To Arms* (Oxford UP, 2001). Acclaimed first volume of a comprehensive history of the war.

John Terraine, *The Great War 1914–1918* (Wordsworth Military Classics, 1998)

Official histories

After the war the government commissioned teams of historians to prepare detailed official histories of the war, formally known as the *History of the Great War based on Official Documents*. There are separate multi-volume series for each year on the Western Front and for the Royal Navy, the War in the Air and for certain civilian functions. Because of their specialist nature they tend to be hard going for the novice, although they are essential for understanding how a unit's activities fitted into the bigger picture. Many reference libraries will have incomplete sets. The IWM and the Naval and Military Press have published reprints of many volumes. The IWM has a complete set, while the Library of the National Archives has odd volumes. Other libraries may also have incomplete sets.

124

In addition most regiments and corps have published semi-official histories outlining their activities during the war. The most complete set of these histories is held by the Imperial War Museum, although the Society of Genealogists also has a good collection. Local libraries are likely to have volumes for local units. These volumes are listed in Roger Perkins, *Regiments: Regiments and Corps of the British Empire and Commonwealth 1758–1993: a Critical Bibliography of their Published Histories* (David and Charles, 1994) and Arthur S. White, *A Bibliography of Regimental Histories of the British Army* (London, Stamp Exchange, 1988). Both volumes have been published on CD as *Armies of the Crown* (Naval and Military Press). However, you can find many volumes listed in Norman Holding's *The Location of British Army Records 1914–1918* (together with where they can be found) and on-line at www.armymuseums.org.uk.

ARMY

Reference

Norman Holding, *The Location of British Army Records, 1914–1918* (4th edition, Federation of Family History Societies, 1999)

Norman Holding, *More Sources of World War I Ancestry* (3rd edition, Federation of Family History Societies, 1998)

Imperial War Museum, *Tracing your Family History: Army* (IWM, 2000)

S.B. and D.B. Jarvis, *The Cross of Sacrifice: Officers Who Died in the Service of the British, Indian and East African Regiments and Corps, 1914–1919* (Naval and Military Press, 1993)

S.B. and D.B. Jarvis, *The Cross of Sacrifice: Officers Who Died in the Service of the Commonwealth and Colonial Regiments and Corps, 1914–1919* (Naval and Military Press, 2000)

William Spencer, *Army Service Records of the First World War* (PRO Publications, 2001)

William Spencer and Simon Fowler, *Army Records for Family History* (PRO Publications, 1998)

General reading

Max Arthur, *Forgotten Voices of the First World War* (Ebury Press, 2002)

Tony Ashworth, *Trench Warfare 1914–1918: The Live and Let Live System* (Macmillan, 1980)

Ilana R. Bet-El, *Conscripts: Lost Legions of the Great War* (Sutton Publishing, 1999)

Malcolm Brown, *The Imperial War Museum Book of the Western Front* (Pan, 2001)

Malcolm Brown, *Tommy Goes to War* (Tempus, 2001)

Richard Holmes, *The Western Front: Ordinary Soldiers and the Defining Battles of World War I* (TV Books, 2000)

Lyn Macdonald, *1914: The Days of Hope* (Penguin, 1989)

Lyn Macdonald, *1915: The Death of Innocence* (Penguin, 1997)

Lyn Macdonald, *1914–1918 Voices and Images of the First World War* (Penguin, 1991)

Lyn Macdonald, *The Somme* (Penguin, 1993)

Lyn Macdonald, *They Called It Passchendaele: The Story of the Third Battle of Ypres and of the Men Who Fought in It* (Penguin, 1993)

Lyn Macdonald, *To the Last Man: Spring 1918* (Penguin, 1999)

Martin Middlebrook, *The First Day on the Somme* (Penguin, 2001)

Martin Middlebrook, *The Kaiser's Battle* (Penguin, 2000)

Richard van Emden, *The Trench* (Bantam, 2002)

Denis Winter, *Death's Men: Soldiers of the Great War* (Penguin, 1979)

NAVY

Reference

Imperial War Museum, *Tracing Your Family History: Royal Navy* (IWM, 1999)

S.B. and D.B. Jarvis, *The Cross of Sacrifice: Non-Commissioned Officers, Men and Women of the UK, Commonwealth and Empire Who Died in the Service of the Royal Naval Air Service, Royal Navy, Royal Marines, Royal Flying Corps and Royal Air Force 1914–1921* (Naval and Military Press, 1996)

Bruno Pappalardo, *Tracing Your Naval Ancestors* (PRO Publications, 2003)

General reading

Max Arthur, *The True Glory: The Royal Navy: 1914–1939* (Hodder and Stoughton, 1996)

Richard Hough, *The Great War at Sea* (Oxford University Press, 1983)

Peter H. Liddle, *The Sailor's War 1914–1918* (Blandford Press, 1985)

AIR SERVICES

Reference

Simon Fowler et al, *RAF Records in the PRO* (Public Record Office, 1994)

Norman Franks, *Who Downed the Aces in WWI?: Facts, Figures and Photos on the Fate of Over 300 Top Pilots of the RFC, RNAS, RAF, French and German Air Services* (Grub Street, 1996)

Norman Franks, Russell Guest and Gregory Alegri, *Above the War Fronts: A Complete Record of the British Two-seater Bomber Pilot and Observer Aces, the British Two-seater Fighter Observer Aces, and the Belgian, Italian, Austro-Hungarian and Russian Fighter Aces, 1914–1918* (Grub Street, 1997)

T. Henshaw, *The Sky Their Battlefield* (Grub Street, 1995). Also includes information on the daily operations of First World War squadrons.

Imperial War Museum, *Tracing Your Family History: Royal Air Force* (IWM, 2000)

S.B. and D.B. Jarvis, *The Cross of Sacrifice: Non-Commissioned Officers, Men and Women of the UK, Commonwealth and Empire Who Died in the Service of the Royal Naval Air Service, Royal Navy, Royal Marines, Royal Flying Corps and Royal Air Force 1914–1921* (Naval and Military Press, 1996)

I. McInnes, J.V. Webb, *Contemptible Little Flying Corps* (Military and Naval Press, 2001). About the early days of the Royal Flying Corps.

Christopher Shores and Mark Rolfe, *British and Empire Aces of World War I (Aircraft of the Aces)* (Osprey, 2001)

Christopher Shores, Norman Franks and Russell Guest, *Above the Trenches. A Complete Record of the Fighter Aces and Units of the British Empire Air Forces, 1915–1920* (Grub Street, 1995 with a supplement published in 1996)

William Spencer, *Air Force Records for Family Historians* (PRO Publications, 2002)

General reading

Cecil Lewis, *Sagittarius Rising* (Penguin, 1977). Probably the best known (and many would argue the best) account of life in the RFC during the First World War.

MERCHANT NAVY

Reference

Imperial War Museum, *Tracing your Family History: Merchant Navy* (IWM, 2000)

S.B. and D.B. Jarvis, *The Cross of Sacrifice: Officers, Men and Women of the Merchant Navy and Mercantile Fleet Auxiliary, 1914–1919* (Naval and Military Press, 2000)

Kelvin Smith et al, *Records of Merchant Shipping and Seamen* (PRO Publications, 1998)

Chris and Michael Watts, *My Ancestor was a Merchant Seaman* (2nd edition, Society of Genealogists, 2002)

CIVILIAN LIFE

General reading

Gail Baybon and Penny Summerfield, *Out of the Cage: Women's Experiences in Two World Wars* (Pandora, 1987)

Diana Condell and Jenny Liddiard, *Working for Victory? Images of women in the First World War, 1914–18* (Routledge and Kegan Paul, 1987)

Gerard J. de Groot, *Blighty: British Society in the Era of the Great War* (Longman, 1996)

Lyn Macdonald, *The Roses of No Man's Land* (London, 1993)

Arthur Marwick, *The Deluge* (2nd edition, Macmillan, 1991)

Arthur Marwick, *Women at War, 1914–1918* (Imperial War Museum, 1977)

E.S. Turner, *Dear Old Blighty* (Michael Joseph, 1980)

There are a large number of local histories of towns and villages during the war. Some were published in the 1920s and 1930s (including volumes for Chester, Croydon, and Portsmouth), while many have been published in the past few years. One of the best of the modern crop is Chris Howell, *No Thankful Village* (Fickle Hill, 2002).

Magazines

There are several magazines devoted to military history, which regularly include articles about the First World War notably *The Great War Magazine*, which is published by Great Northern Publishing, PO Box 202, Scarborough YO11 3GE (www.greatnorthernpublishing.co.uk/the-great-war.htm). There are also a number of smaller, more specialist journals such as *Gunfire* (available from Dr Alf Peacock,126 Holgate Rd, York YO24 4DL or visit www.ghsmith.com/worldwar1/gunfire.html) and

Firestep (Arthur Potton, 42 Glenalla Rd, Ruislip HA4 5DL). Other military and family history magazines also regularly publish articles, certainly *Family History Monthly* does.

Book publishers
Publishers of military books about the First World War include: Naval & Military Press, Unit 10, Ridgewood Industrial Park, Uckfield TN22 5QE; tel: 01825 749494; www.naval-military-press.com. Has an active publishing programme, mainly CD-ROMS and reprints of official publications and official histories. They also sell books relating to warfare that are described in regular catalogues sent to subscribers. It is worth subscribing as the catalogues provide a reasonable guide to what is in print and often contain books at a discounted price.

Pen & Sword Books Ltd, 47 Church St, Barnsley S70 2AS; tel: 01226 734555; www.pen-and-sword.co.uk. Also publishes books under the Leo Cooper imprint.

Sutton Publishing, Phoenix Mill, Thrupp, Stroud GL5 2BU; tel: 01453 731114; www.suttonpublishing.co.uk.

Bookshops will order any book in print for you, provided (naturally) you know the name of the author and title. You can also order titles on-line at www.amazon.co.uk and www.historybookshop.com. There are also a number of specialist military booksellers, of whom the best known is probably Ray Westlake, 53 Claremont, Malpas, Newport NP20 6PL.

Second hand books
There are a number of specialist dealers in books of the First World War. Among them are:

Battlefront Books
17 Downsway Close
Tadworth
KT2 5DR
www.battlefrontbooks.com

David J. Harrison
19 Conway Rd
London
SW20 8PA

Appendix V
WEBSITES

॰ॐ

The First World War and the internet seem to have a natural affinity judging by the hundreds of sites there are on the war. Some are very professional with hundreds of pages of material, while others may just be about an individual man, a unit or a hospital. The sites listed below are a selection of general ones about the war. More specialist sites are mentioned in the appropriate place in the main body of the text.

REFERENCE

www.1914–1918.net/home.htm	A general site dedicated to the British Army in the First World War
www.bbc.co.uk/history/war/ wwone/index.shtml	The BBC's impressive guide to the First World War. It's what our licence money goes on!
www.fylde.demon.co.uk/ welcome.htm	Hellfire Corner, a variety of interesting pages with a British and Commonwealth angle, particularly relating to battlefield tourism and memorials.
www.geocities.com/ ~worldwar1/default.html	A curious Dutch site devoted to the heritage of the War with some very interesting perspectives. A not dissimilar site (although with better graphics) is www.unfortunate-region.org.
www.geocities.com/Athens/ Acropolis/2354/	This site dedicated to a group of re-enactors also has a number of

www.great-war-research-services.com/links.htm	useful pages on the British Army and its organisation during the war. The site mainly advertises a research service on the war, but there are some excellent links to other sites. Unusually for WW1 sites (which are in general poorly designed) it's also attractively laid out.
www.hcu.ox.ac.uk/mirrors/ www.lib.byu.edu:80/~rdh/wwi/index.html	The WW1 Document Archive reproduces documents pertinent to the war. Has useful links to specialist genealogical or bio-graphical sites.
www.oldcontemptible.com	About the Old Contemptibles, that is the British soldiers who fought in France between August and November 1914. When I visited, it was still very much under construction.
www.regiments.org	Land Forces of the British Empire and Commonwealth – devoted to the history of units of the British Army and daughter armies across the globe since the 18th century. Particularly useful as a reference tool with links to more specialist sites.
www.worldwar1.com/	Excellent American site devoted to the war although with an American bias. It can be a tad confusing navigating around.
www.yfd59.dial.pipex.com	About Kitchener's Armies, the men who volunteered for service during 1914 and 1915, with some useful pages about sources.
http://battlefields1418.50megs.com/main_menu.htm	The Old Front Line – mainly provides help and guidance to people wishing to visit the battle-fields. Some interesting pages.

www.firstworldwar.com	Superb and very attractive site designed largely with schools in mind with many pages devoted to aspects of the war, including battlefield tourism, recordings of contemporary songs, and posters and photographs.
www.gwpda.org	A site containing copies of documents and other material about the First World War. There are also some useful pages relating to the history at sea.
www.hellotommy.co.uk	The aim of this site is to sell tours to the Western Front, although there are some useful pages about touring and links to other web sites.
www.kev84.worldonline.co.uk/soldiersdied.html	
	A free research service for men who died during the war.
www.pitt.edu/~pugachev/greatwar/toc.htm	
	An excellent site with pages devoted to many aspects of the war, including researching servicemen and Ireland's role in the conflict.

Appendix VI

LIST OF ABBREVIATIONS

❧

You will almost certainly come across abbreviations in war diaries and other official papers. Here are some of the most common.

2/Lt	Second Lieutenant
ADS	Advanced Dressing Station
AEF	American Expeditionary Force
AIF	Australian Imperial Force
ANZAC	Australian and New Zealand Army Corps
ASC	Army Service Corps
AVC	Army Veterinary Corps
Bde	Brigade
BEF	British Expeditionary Force
Bn or Btn	Battalion
BSM	Battery Sergeant Major
CCS	Casualty Clearing Station
Cdr	Commander
CEF	Canadian Expeditionary Force
CinC	Commander in Chief
CO	Commanding Officer
Coy	Regimental company
Cpl	Corporal
Cpt or Capt	Captain
CSM	Company Sergeant Major
Div	Division
DoW	Died of wounds
Drv	Driver
F&F	France and Flanders (i.e. Western Front)
FA	Field Ambulance
FOO	Forward Observation Officer (controlled artillery fire)

Ft	Flight
GHQ	General headquarters
Gnr	Gunner
GOC	General Officer Commanding
GSW	Gun shot wound
HE	High Explosive
KiA	Killed in Action
L of C	Lines of Communication
L/Bdr	Lance Bombardier (Royal Artillery)
L/Cpl	Lance Corporal
Lt or Lieut	Lieutenant
MC	Military Cross
Med	Medium
MEF	Mediterranean Expeditionary Force
MG	Machine Gun
MGC	Machine Gun Corps
MM	Military Medal
NCO	Non-Commissioned Officer
OP	Observation Post
OR	Other Ranks
PoW	Prisoner of War
Pte	Private
RA	Royal Artillery
RAF	Royal Air Force
RE	Royal Engineers
RFA	Royal Field Artillery
RFC	Royal Flying Corps
RGA	Royal Garrison Artillery
RHA	Royal Horse Artillery
RM	Royal Marines
RNAS	Royal Naval Air Service
RND	Royal Naval Division
RNR	Royal Naval Reserve
RNVR	Royal Naval Volunteer Reserve
RSM	Regimental Sergeant Major
Sgt	Sergeant
Sig	Signal
Spr	Sapper (Royal Engineers)
TMB	Trench Mortar Battery
Trp	Trooper
W or wd	Wounded

Appendix VII

ARMY COMMAND STRUCTURE

❧

ARMY
Largest sub-division of the British Army (250,000–350,000 men) commanded by a general.

CORPS
Each army was split into three to six corps; each corps normally had four divisions commanded by a lieutenant general.

There were also specialist corps, most notably the Royal Artillery and Royal Engineers, but also medical, veterinary and service. Typically they were divided into companies commanded by a captain or major.

DIVISION
Each division had roughly 18,000 men, 4,000 horses, 850 wagons. Commanded by a major general.

BRIGADE
Sub-division of a division (typically there were three or four brigades in each division). It was commanded by a brigadier general. There were also artillery brigades which were split into four batteries.

REGIMENT
Before 1916 regiments were largely recruited from a specific locality and so built up close links with a particular district. There were normally two battalions, one stationed at home with the other overseas, normally India, with one or two additional territorial or volunteer battalions made up of part-time soldiers. During the war the regiment had a much less fixed role, perhaps providing basic training at the

regimental depot, a focus for local charitable effort sending parcels to men of the regiment at the front or in prisoner of war camps, and acting as a focal point for loyalty from men and officers alike.

BATTALION
In peacetime a regiment comprised between one and four battalions – during the war there could be ten battalions or more scattered along the front line or on other theatres of operation or training in Britain. They comprised of between 800 and 1000 men and were commanded by a colonel.

COMPANY
There were four companies per infantry battalion consisting of between 100 and 400 men or a unit of corps. They were commanded by a major or captain.

PLATOON
There were four per company (30–50 men), typically commanded by a lieutenant or second lieutenant.

SECTION
Four per platoon (10–15 men), commanded by a sergeant or corporal. Example:

ONE MAN'S PLACE IN THE WAR
V Army (Flanders 1915)
↑

59th (2nd North Middlesex Division)
↑

2/8 Sherwood Foresters
↑

A Company
↑

1 Section
↑

Individual soldier (ie 306983 Lance Corporal T.E. Borrill)

(Based on table in David Borrill, *Great War Family Ancestry Resource Booklet*)

Comparative rank structure between the various services

Officers

Army	Navy	RNAS	RAF
	Midshipman		
Second Lieutenant	Sub Lieutenant	Flight Sub Lieutenant	Pilot Officer
Lieutenant	Lieutenant	Flight Lieutenant	Flying Officer
Captain	Lieutenant	Flight Commander	Flight Lieutenant
Major	Lieutenant Commander	Squadron Commander	Squadron Leader
Lieutenant Colonel	Commander	Wing Commander	Wing Commander
Colonel	Captain		Group Captain
Brigadier General	Commodore		Air Commodore
Major General	Rear Admiral		Air Vice Marshal
Lieutenant General	Vice Admiral		Air Marshal
General	Admiral		Air Chief Marshal
Field Marshal	Admiral of the Fleet		Marshal of the RAF

Non-commissioned officers and other ranks:

Army	Navy	RAF
Private/Gunner/ Bombadier/Sapper	Rating	Aircraftsman
Lance Corporal	Leading Rating	Leading Aircraftsman
Corporal	Petty Officer	Corporal
Sergeant	Chief Petty Officer	Sergeant
Sergeant Major	Warrant Officer	Flight Sergeant

RAF ranks were not adopted until 1919. During 1918 the new service used Army ranks. The exact terminology for Army other ranks varied slightly between regiments and corps.

Service numbers

Service, or regimental, numbers can be confusing. Until late in 1918 a soldier was assigned a new number every time he joined a new regiment. These regimental numbers began at no 1 in the early 1880s and were assigned numerically, so the lower the number a man had the earlier he had joined up. However, from the middle of 1916 soldiers began to be transferred between regiments to reinforce or rebuild units which had been devastated during battle. This was often very unpopular with the men themselves. Where this happened soldiers were allocated a new regimental number. So, during a man's service he might have two or three such numbers. However, an Army-wide system was introduced in late 1918, whereby a man was assigned a single number which remained with him during his service.

The Royal Navy had a different system, which was based on the branch or trade (engineering, gunnery and so on) to which a rating belonged. The branch was indicated by an initial letter or letters before the Continuous Service Number. A list is given in Bruno Pappalardo, *Tracing Your Naval Ancestors* (PRO, 2003) and in the NA leaflet *Royal Navy: Ratings' Service Records* 1667–1923 (Military Records Information 31), which can be downloaded from their website.

On its formation in April 1918 the RAF used a simple numerical system.

Appendix VIII

TIME LINE

Key Events during the First World War

1914

28 July – Austria Hungary declares war on Serbia

4 Aug – Britain declares war on Germany

10 Aug – Arrival of first British troops in France

22 Aug – First British military engagement of the war near Mons in Southern Belgium

23 Aug – Death of first British soldier in action (Pte J. Parr, Middlesex Regiment) at Mons

5–10 Sept – Battle of the Marne

9 Oct – Germans capture Antwerp, capturing thousands of Royal Marines

30 Oct–24 Nov – First Battle of Ypres

6 Nov – Britain declares war on Turkey

16 Dec – German fleet shells Scarborough and Hartlepool

25 Dec – Christmas truce on Western Front

1915

19 Jan – First Zeppelin raid on Britain

4 Feb – German submarine attacks on merchant shipping begins

10–15 Mar – Battle of Neuve Chappelle

22 Apr–14 May – Second Battle of Ypres

22 Apr – First use of poison gas on Western Front

25 Apr – Landing of Australian and New Zealand Army Corps at Gallipoli

23 May – Italy enters war on Allied side

25 Sept–5 Oct – Battle of Loos and Champagne

9 Oct – British and French troops land at Salonica, Greece

7 Dec – Siege of British and Indian troops at Kut begins

17 Dec – Sir Douglas Haig replaces Sir John French as commander of the British Expeditionary Force

1916

27 Jan – Military Service Act introduces conscription

21 Feb–18 December – Battle of Verdun

23 April – Easter Rising in Dublin

29 April – British troops surrender at Kut, the worst British military disaster until the Fall of Singapore in 1942.

31 May–1 June – Battle of Jutland

1 July–18 Nov – First Battle of the Somme

15 July–3 Sept – Battle of Delville Wood

23–3 Sept – Battle of Pozieres

10 Sept–19 Nov – Allied offensive at Salonika

15 Sept – First use of tanks on Western Front

13–18 Nov – Battle of the Ancre

7 Dec – David Lloyd George replaces Herbert Asquith as British Prime Minister

1917

23 Feb–5 April – German retreat to Hindenburg Line

12 March – First Russian Revolution

6 April – United States declares war on Germany

9 April–3 May – Battle of Arras

9–14 April – Battle of Vimy Ridge

10 May – British introduce convoy system

7–14 June – Battle of Messines

26 June – First American troops land in France

31 July–10 Nov – Third Battle of Ypres (Passchendaele)

4 Nov – British troops arrive in Italy

7 Nov – Second Russian Revolution: Bolsheviks seize power

20 Nov–3 Dec – Battle of Cambrai

2 Dec – Ceasefire on Eastern Front

9 Dec – British capture Jerusalem from the Turks

1918

8 Jan – Fourteen points peace plan outlined by President Wilson

3 March – Peace treaty of Brest-Litovsk between Germany and the Bolsheviks

21 March – Start of German advance on Western Front 'Operation Michael'

21 March–4 April – Second Battle of the Somme

9–29 April – Battle of the Lys

1 June – American troops drive back Germans at Chateau-Thierry

20–31 July – Battle of the Marne

5–18 Aug – Start of the 'Hundred Days' with the advance in Flanders

24 Aug–3 Sept – Third Battle of the Somme

18 Sept–9 Oct – Battle of the Hindenburg Line

17 Oct – Occupation of Lille

3 Nov – Armistice with Austria-Hungary

11 Nov – Armistice with Germany

11 Nov – Death of last British soldier in action (Pte G.E. Ellison, 5th Royal Lancers). He is buried at Saint Symphorien Cemetery, Mons near the first British casualty of the war (see 23 August 1914)

21 Nov – German High Seas Fleet surrenders to British

1919

4 Jan – Peace conference convenes in Paris

21 June – German High Seas Fleet scuttled at Scarpa Flow

28 June – Germany signs Treaty of Versailles

21 July – Britain signs Treaty of Versailles

INDEX

142

144